Grief
And
Comforting the Grieving

How Should the Christian Respond to Grief?

By
Karl Crawford

All Scripture References are from the King James Bible

PineTree Ministries
906 Eppler Road
Petoskey, Michigan 49770
karl@pinetreeministries.org

Contents

Preface

This study is written for two groups: for those who are presently grieving and for those who desire to minister to them. It assumes that the one grieving and the one desiring to minister to those in grief know the Lord as Personal Savior. If you do not know Jesus Christ as Personal Saviour, if you are not sure for Scriptural reasons that you will spend eternity in heaven when you die please see the plan of salvation in the Appendix of this book.

Grief is not a topic to be studied as much as an experience to be lived. While we may experience the same reasons to grieve—death, extreme loss, terminal disease, we will all grieve through them differently. But while your grief may manifest itself differently than my grief the Scriptural remedies are the same for both of us.

This study moves back and forth between those currently grieving and those desiring to minister. You will find this study is applicable for you in whichever circumstance you find yourself.

I have included a few "Songs" that I wrote a number of years ago when I was in the depths of my own grief. I found help in the Psalms of the Old Testament and thought that if it helped the Psalmist to write their words of frustration and praise to God then I should do so as well. I couldn't call them Psalms and have someone think I was comparing my writings to the Scriptures so I called them "Songs" instead. They have no worth other than to help me put my grief into words and to help me understand myself a little better. Since writing these "Songs" twenty years ago I have shared them with only a few people; I am giving you a peek into my life at a very vulnerable time—please think of them accordingly.

Throughout this study I have included many true stories as examples to discuss. Names have been changed to protect identities. These are more than classroom examples—these are real people who have been impacted by grief, some of them changed for the better and some for the worse, but each of them forever changed.

I don't offer this study as the definitive work on grieving. I am not an expert, I don't always grieve very well myself. However, I believe that the Word of God is the final authority on how a Christian should grieve and how to minister to others. It is my intention to point you to the Scriptures.

My goal in presenting this study is to help the Body of Christ to grow and prosper by encouraging and enabling individual believers. My prayer for everyone who reads this is to:

◊ Know and comprehend that God is good and that He loves you personally.

◊ Know that God has a plan and a purpose for you; that you identify the purpose and begin to live it out.

◊ Know that God is in control and He is still good and worthy of your praise regardless of what trials you may be facing.

◊ Move to minister to those in grief; to help them begin to see the Light and the comfort from the True Comforter and to help others see the necessity to minister to the grieving.

I have told those with whom I have shared this study that there are two truths that, if they truly learn them, I will feel as though I have succeeded. The first truth is that God is in control. The second truth is that God is good. Romans 8:28 is a verse that we treat far too lightly. It plainly teaches that God is in control, how else can He promise to work 'all things' together for good for His children?

Note

It is very important that you read the Scriptures included in this study. I know there are many of them and sometimes we have a tendency to skip over them. Let me say that if you are only going to read portions of this study—read the Scriptures. You will move through life just fine if you never hear a word I have to say however you will miss God if you do not read the Scripture references.

SONG 207

1. Death. A scary, bone-chilling word that strikes fear to the core of our being, to the bottom of our heart.

2. We have an idea of what life means, we have a familiarity with it. We sometimes hate life with its trials and pain, but we still cling to it. No matter how bad life gets, it is still better than death, better than the unknown.

3. We know we have hope, as Your children, for this life and for the life beyond. But as much as we like to talk about and sing about that hope, we don't look forward to death, to the vehicle that transports us to the reality of our hope.

4. We need You Lord, to walk with us through the dark valley of death. It is a fearful time for us, scaring us - pardon the expression - to death.

5. But You are our refuge Lord, the only Refuge for us when we are troubled with the cares and trials of this life.

6. But even more now, in this time of the darkness of death, we need You and You alone to walk with us.

7. We are fearful Lord - calm our hearts.

8. We are scared Lord - take our hands and give us peace.

9. We are safe Lord - in this life and the one to come - when we are in Your hands, by Your side - on our way home.

The Author

I have worked at Greenwood Cemetery in Petoskey since June of 1961. My grandfather began there as superintendent in 1920. My father began working for his father in 1930 and became superintendent not too long after that. When my dad retired in 1977, I became the superintendent. In my years at Greenwood and in associated businesses I have been involved with, or responsible for, more than 7,000 funerals. I also have been faced with the deaths of many close family members and friends—experiencing funerals not as a professional but as a reluctant participant.

I don't present this study from the role of a pastor or other authority. I am a cemeterian, an observant observer, but most of all, I am a Christian who has been impressed by the Lord with the need to care for His children and also for those who are not of the faith at a very difficult time in their life. God has blessed me with trials that have caused me to experience grief and He has blessed me with His comfort which has helped heal the scars left by that grief. It is from that perspective that I present these thoughts.

It was during my own time of grief that the Lord caused me to read and understand in a way I had not previously grasped the Apostle Paul's words in 2 Corinthians regarding the process of suffering.

2 Corinthians 1:3-7 Blessed be God, even the Father of our Lord Jesus Christ, the Father of mercies, and the God of all comfort; Who comforteth us in all our tribulation, that we may be able to comfort them which are in any trouble, by the comfort wherewith we ourselves are comforted of God. For as the sufferings of Christ abound in us, so our consolation also aboundeth by Christ. And whether we be afflicted, it is for your consolation and salvation, which is effectual in the enduring of the same sufferings which we also suffer: or whether we be comforted, it is for your consolation and salvation. And our hope of you is stedfast, knowing, that as ye are partakers of the sufferings, so shall ye be also of the consolation.

"*Blessed be God*" Paul says, who gives us comfort in "*all our tribulation*" so that we may be able to comfort others. And I say thanks be to God who blesses us with comfort and then blesses us again with purpose— to in turn give that comfort to others.

Karl

Chapter 1

The Face of Grief

Introduction

Grief is something that only the masochists among us enjoy but it is something that most all of us will face at some point in our life. Some may be consumed by the grief of graduating second in their class in high school when they knew they were smart enough to be first—few of us can identify with their grief. Some may face the grief of the death of multiple children and live out the remainder of their life with no close family. None of us want to be able to identify with their grief.

This study is for those suffering through grief and for those whom the Lord has called on to help them in their grief. If you don't think the Lord has called you to walk with those who are going through a debilitating time in their life and you are a Christian— you are wrong. Each one of us is called to *"weep with them that weep."* [1] We may like the other half of

---

1 Romans 12:15 Rejoice with them that do rejoice, and weep with them that weep.

that verse more, to *"rejoice with them that do rejoice"* but we are not given the choice. Each of us is given the ministry of walking alongside those for whom, at this point in their journey, life seems too difficult to manage.

What Is Grief?

Webster's Dictionary of 1828 defines the word grief as: *"The pain of mind produced by loss, misfortune, injury or evils of any kind; sorrow; regret. We experience grief when we lose a friend, when we incur loss, when we consider ourselves injured, and by sympathy, we feel grief at the misfortunes of others."* [2]

The above definition may satisfy the inquiring mind but it does not satisfy the heart—it is much too sterile. We don't need to go to a dictionary to know that grief means more than *"pain of mind."* Our heart tells us that grief is 'a pain in our heart that won't go away;' 'an ever-present ache in our bones'; 'a mind that is overwhelmed with thoughts yet unable to express them' or a mind that is unable to think at all. We know that grief takes a normally functioning life and places it on an interminable hold, seemingly with no way back to 'normal.'

Jeremiah wrote the following words in 586 B.C. at the destruction of Jerusalem. I have highlighted some of his words of grief:

> *Lamentations 1:12-22 Is it nothing to you, all ye that pass by? behold, and <u>see if there be any sorrow like unto my sorrow</u>, which is done unto me, wherewith the LORD hath afflicted me in the day of his fierce anger. From above hath <u>he sent fire into my bones</u>, and it prevaileth against them: he hath spread a net for my feet, he hath*

2 Webster' Dictionary, 1828, Online Edition

turned me back: he hath made me desolate and faint all the day. The yoke of my transgressions is bound by his hand: they are wreathed, and come up upon my neck: he hath made my strength to fall, the Lord hath delivered me into their hands, from whom I am not able to rise up. The Lord hath trodden under foot all my mighty men in the midst of me: he hath called an assembly against me to crush my young men: the Lord hath trodden the virgin, the daughter of Judah, as in a winepress. For these things I weep; mine eye, mine eye runneth down with water, because the comforter that should relieve my soul is far from me: my children are desolate, because the enemy prevailed. Zion spreadeth forth her hands, and there is none to comfort her: the LORD hath commanded concerning Jacob, that his adversaries should be round about him: Jerusalem is as a menstruous woman among them. The LORD is righteous; for I have rebelled against his commandment: hear, I pray you, all people, and behold my sorrow: my virgins and my young men are gone into captivity. I called for my lovers, but they deceived me: my priests and mine elders gave up the ghost in the city, while they sought their meat to relieve their souls. Behold, O LORD; for I am in distress: my bowels are troubled; mine heart is turned within me; for I have grievously rebelled: abroad the sword bereaveth, at home there is as death. They have heard that I sigh: there is none to comfort me: all mine enemies have heard of my trouble; they are glad that thou hast done it: thou wilt bring the day that thou hast called, and they shall be like unto me. Let all their wickedness come before thee; and do unto them, as thou hast done unto me for all my transgressions: for my sighs are many, and my heart is faint.

Jeremiah is describing God's judgment for Israel's sin. I am not saying nor even implying that sin is the reason you are facing a time of grief but anyone experiencing grief will be able to relate to Jeremiah's words. Jeremiah asks if anyone has ever known sorrow like his, he is desolate and faint all the day, he weeps and believes his Comforter is far from him and he feels oppressed by his enemies, abandoned by his friends and afflicted by His Lord. His enemies are glad that he is in travail, his bowels are troubled, his sighs are many and his heart is faint.

A mother was telling me about the pain in her heart caused by a wayward daughter. She said she felt as though her heart "was literally breaking in two." She said it a few times so I could grasp that she really felt like it was breaking. It was not a trite phrase, it was the reality of her grief.

Grief can cause healthy widows or widowers to die a few weeks or months after their spouse because they cannot face life alone. An evangelist and his wife spent 45 years in the ministry. He preached the Gospel for all of those years but when his wife died he was a broken man. He didn't take care of himself physically or emotionally and died of a broken heart 4½ years later. His death

In grief there is always a death. It may be a death of someone we loved, an important figure in our life (pastor, favorite school teacher, president), it may be the death of our job, divorce, a child's failing or a financial reversal. In these latter things, while there is not a physical death, there is a death of a portion of our self—a dying back of a little bit of who we are or think we are. There is a death of pride or satisfaction. There is a death of one of our safe places—better, a death of one of our gods.

10

was no honor to her memory nor was it an honor to God to say to the Father and to anyone watching that God was not enough for whatever this new period in this preacher's life was to be.

What Does Grief Look Like?

Grief may be experienced in many different forms and at many different levels.

◊ The pregnant young wife who just received the word that her husband has been killed. She is facing the birth and raising of their baby without the baby's father present.

◊ The man whose wife is killed by some hot-rodding teenagers and who learns a few years later that his son and four grandchildren have been killed in a plane crash.

◊ The wife of a 100 year-old man. Their marriage of 73+ years came to an end with his death. Just because she has been married more years than many people have been alive does not mean she does not grieve. They have outlived their friends, she has few to comfort her.

◊ A young woman whose mom died. A few years later her father remarried. His second wife hates the only daughter and makes life as difficult for her as possible. When her father died the daughter needed help with the grief of losing her father but also with the difficulties of dealing with a mean and spiteful stepmother. The daughter does not even know for sure where her father is buried and she never will. The death of the evil stepmother does little to lessen the young woman's heartache.

◊ A daughter who throws herself across her mother's casket and wails, "Mom, don't leave me. I love you Mom. Don't leave me."

◊ The young mother, obviously pregnant, who came to the cemetery alone to pick out a place to bury the baby that was dead inside her womb. The funeral would have to wait until the following week because the hospital would not take the baby until the 'scheduled day for doing that type of operation.'

◊ The mother whose 2 day-old baby died who says, "If that is the kind of God I serve I want nothing to do with Him." And she didn't.

◊ A 55 year-old man works long hours at a hospital. He is the 'go to' guy for all that happens in construction and maintenance and does his job well, working on holidays and weekends to make sure that projects are going smoothly. He is called to the office one day to find that he is without a job. One minute he is the dedicated employee and a few minutes later he is escorted to his car by a security guard—a victim of budget cuts.

◊ A woman in her 70s whose husband had passed away years ago visited a cemetery to purchase a single burial plot—for herself. Her only son was dying in California from a terminal disease and she had no one to come with her. She was faced with making all of the arrangements for her own death—alone.

◊ A friend whose husband came home from work one day to tell her he was leaving her and their three children—for his gay lover.

◊ A woman whose 13 year-old son died 33 years ago still can barely talk about his death without shedding tears. She is a healthy, strong woman. She has other children and loves them dearly. Yet that young son who died of cancer left a permanent hole in her heart that refuses to be filled in this life. It is not morbid—it is grief.

◊ The husband of a wife of 47 years. He pulled out in front of a county snowplow which struck their car broadside and his wife died instantly. He knows that her death was his fault. The driver of the snowplow was her stepbrother and he has his own grief to deal with. Adding guilt to grief only makes recovery more difficult.

◊ A man whose cancer forced him to have his leg amputated below the knee. He handled that well including learning how to live with a prosthetic. His desolation came when the cancer returned, forcing more leg to be amputated and raising doubt whether this is the last time he would experience this or not.

◊ The woman in her late thirties whose husband had after so many years of depression committed suicide. His bouts of depression and subsequent hospitalization were difficult to deal with but there was always hope that counseling or medication would work and life would be as they both wanted it to be. When he committed suicide in the basement of their home hope was replaced by grief.

How would you react if you faced the same loss as one of the above persons? What would you say to a fellow church member who is facing any one of the above examples of loss? Would you tell them to pull up their 'big boy pants' and move on with life? Would you tell them that one year is long enough to grieve? How would you weep with them as they weep? And how long would you grieve with them?

> *1 Corinthians 12:25-26 That there should be no schism in the body; but that the members should have the same care one for another. And whether one member suffer, all the members suffer with it; or one member be honoured, all the members rejoice with it.*

> *Romans 12:15-16 Rejoice with them that do rejoice, and weep with them that weep. Be of the same mind one toward another. Mind not high things, but condescend to men of low estate. Be not wise in your own conceits.*

To *"be not wise in your own conceits"* means for our study that we are to be careful not to judge how someone else is grieving by how we think we would grieve if we were in the same situation. Far too many times in my life I have said verbally or to myself, "I would never react the way that person is reacting" only to have God give me the opportunity to experience the same trial as the person I was judging. I have a perfect record in having to eat my words every time I judged people without knowing their circumstances. Rather than condemning them we are to rejoice with the rejoicers and we are to grieve with the grievers. We are to help them carry their burden while pointing them to the Father.

> Zephaniah 3:17 The Lord thy God in the midst of thee is mighty; He will save, he will rejoice over thee with joy; He will rest in his love, he will joy over thee with singing.

Galatians 6:2 Bear ye one another's burdens, and so fulfil the law of Christ.

We normally think of grieving over the death of a loved one as the major, if not the only, form of grief one will face during a lifetime. Sometimes we scoff at people who grieve for other things dismissing it as depression, seeking attention or a sign of their weakness. But there are many 'deaths' we grieve such as the death of our marriage, career, health, self-confidence or the death of an idol (a small 'g' god). It may be a life-ending illness such as Alzheimer's or ALS. It may be grief over an abortion that seemed like the best thing to do at the time. We grieve for children who have gone the way of the Prodigal. We grieve a church split and the fellowship and sense of belonging to something bigger than ourselves that has been lost.

You probably already are thinking of some examples in your past (or your present) that have caused you to experience grief. It is not wrong to grieve them (assuming they were not sin) but it is wrong to grieve them wrongly—in a way that does not ultimately bring honor to our Heavenly Father. (A cheating husband could grieve the fact that he must give up the relationship with his 'lover' to return to his wife and children or lose his share of his wife's inheritance. That grief can never honor God.)

There are varying ways we can react to another's pain. We can ignore it. From our ivory towers we can sit in judgment on how they are dealing with it. Or we can enter into their pain with them. It is our choice how we respond. We may not be able to lessen their pain but we can walk with them on their journey.

Who Does Grief Look Like?

I asked the question in the previous section, "What Does Grief Look Like?" I think we would be much better served to replace the 'what' with 'who.' Imagine the doctor who comes home after a long day at the hospital and his wife asks how his day went. He might reply, "I set two broken arms, one broken leg and treated four cases of the flu. It was brutal." Another way for the doctor to respond would be to say, "I treated a two year-old little girl whose arm was broken by her drunken, abusive father. The father's arm was broken as well when he was resisting arrest. The broken leg belonged to a skier who was home from college. He is the star of the college basketball team and is in his senior season. He will miss his final year of eligibility. The four cases of flu all belonged to the same family, four children under the age of five. Their mom is a single mother who is trying her best to work to support her family. The day care she uses will not take the children because of their sickness and if she has to stay home with them she will lose her job."

The second account is vastly different than the first. When we think about 'what' grief looks like we think of an angry or dour expression. When we think of 'who' grief looks like we begin to see the need to minister. This is why I have chosen to include the stories of actual people in this study, it is too easy to dismiss grief if we do not have a face to put with the trial.

> Faith is put to the ultimate test when death crushes the hope of healing.
>
> Charles Swindoll

I have met with thousands of people in my office and many more in other aspects of my job. It is easy for me to think of them as just one more widow whose husband of almost 50 years has passed away. She may be the fourth widow I have met with so far this week; to me she is one of many. To her, this is the very first time she has had to make arrangements to bury the man to whom she had devoted her life. The travel plans for their fiftieth anniversary cruise will have to be cancelled. She is thinking about the fact that their house is too large for one person and she can't plow the snow from their driveway and mow the lawn anyway. None of their children live in the area so she will probably have to move to be near one of them, that means leaving her only living sibling along with her friends and her church. This lady is not a 'what', she is a 'who' that needs to know that someone cares about her and desires to help her through this traumatic time.

Sometimes we hear pastors say after a particularly rough stretch of dealing with people, "I love the ministry...it is people I can't stand." We smile when we hear that because we have our own frustrations with people, but it is never God's way. Jesus came to die on the cross because of His great love for people. He didn't die for church buildings or church programs, He didn't die for Christian colleges or camps. He died for people.

In my early years at the cemetery I loved the gardening aspect of my job but didn't care much for dealing with people. When I was made the superintendent and was in charge of all facets of the business, part of my job was meeting with people. I was efficient, pleasant and professional. In my latter years I try to maintain those aspects of my job while adding to it the desire to minister to hurting people. I want them to leave my office feeling better than when they came in. I want their experience in the cemetery to be one that aids their healing process and never hinders it.

In those early years I felt gifted to minister to grass and squirrels and beech trees. My natural bent is to be alone and in a secluded place. Daniel Boone said it was time to move to a new location when you could see smoke from a neighbor's chimney. And yet, Jesus died for people and He calls me to minister to people, not squirrels. It does not matter how well I do the groundskeeping portion of my job if I miss showing Christ. And it doesn't matter how well we comfort hurting people if we do it without showing them Jesus Christ.

> When people come into my office, sometimes the ministry is about me having an impact on them, but sometimes it is about them having an impact on my life. I need to be spiritually ready for either. KC

Grief Can Overwhelm Us

When grief seems to overwhelm us we may be near the point that James Montgomery Boice, in his commentary on Psalm 88[3], speaks of as *"the dark*

---

3 James Montgomery Boice, Psalms Vol. 2, Psalms 42-106, Page 716, Baker Book House

night of the soul." He describes it as, *"a state of intense spiritual anguish in which the struggling despairing believer feels he is abandoned by God."* Think back to Jeremiah's words in the passage from Lamentations; people today feel the same *"intense spiritual anguish"* that he did. It could be you or it could be the one sitting next to you in the pew on Sunday evening who is experiencing that type of grief.

Some never stop talking about how much they are hurting while others refuse to talk about their grief at all. Grief can be worn on our sleeve or buried deep within the crevasses of our soul—but it is still grief, it is still present, and it still changes us. For the Christian this grief must be dealt with; we are not given the option of letting grief define us for the remainder of our life.

◊ Fred is a friend of mine. He is the epitome of the macho individual who cares not if he offends anyone. He is caustic at times and indifferent at others. The casual observer may read many moods into Fred but grief would not be one of them. Yet one day we were traveling together and stopped at a local business. Before I could open the door to get out of the car, he looked over at me and with tears in his eyes, said, "my son would have gotten his driver's license today." I found out later that his son had died at 18 months of age in an automobile accident. Fourteen and one-half years later Fred shed tears of grief over the death of his infant son.

◊ Shirley's husband died unexpectedly at the age of 52. She purchased a cemetery lot, made the burial of her husband of 31 years and began the grieving process. For her the 'process' meant months stretching on into years of visits to the cemetery, sometimes laying out prostrate on her husband's grave "to be close to him." Words and phrases of comfort that helped others meant nothing to her and she could not shake the despair. Years stretched on and she met another man and they married. Even more years later her son died unexpectedly at age 52, and she again experienced grief that sent her deep within herself.

◊ Lydia had a horrible childhood. Her father committed suicide when she was two years old and her mother spent the ensuing years bringing various men into the home—all of them having some sort of role as 'father' to Lydia. She went on to graduate at the top of her high school class but with a promiscuous lifestyle. Lydia married a young man and eventually was led to a saving relationship with Jesus Christ in her 20s. She loves the Lord but, until recently, has lived with an aversion to God in His role as Father. The grief she has lived with from her childhood always stood in the way of her fellowship with God the Father.

Guilt Can Play A Role in Our Grief

Guilt can be a demanding partner to our grief, always reminding us what we should have done, if only.... It is far too easy to get into a never-ending game of 'what-ifs'; believing that if we had done something, anything, we could have prevented the death of that one who was our life.

Adam's sin and my own sin have caused us to have separation from God. Sin has caused mankind corporately and individually to know loss. Because we live in a fallen world human life is a series of losses until we finally enter into heaven's land where losses cease to exist and we find fulfillment in the presence of the Father. Right now we live in the middle—after the fall and before the making right of all things. We live in the time when all of creation has suffered loss—groaning for the coming renewal.[4] We live in the time when loss causes us to know grief and grieving.

Death is a reminder of the loss mankind suffered in the Garden and it should be a reminder that healing or comfort for loss comes to its fullest extent through Jesus Christ. The remedy for the loss in the Garden was not the Law but the Savior. The remedy for the losses we face in this life is only found in the one true Comforter—Jesus Christ. Every other remedy is an ineffective substitute at best.

Anger Can Play A Role in Our Grief

A friend in high school and I reconnected after many years. As we were comparing our spiritual journey from school to retirement he told me that his father left the family when he was 18 months old. He never sent child support, never sent Christmas or birthday gifts and never acknowledged him at all from the age of 18 months. My friend said this has left him with

---

4 Romans 8:22-23 For we know that the whole creation groaneth and travaileth in pain together until now. And not only they, but ourselves also, which have the firstfruits of the Spirit, even we ourselves groan within ourselves, waiting for the adoption, to wit, the redemption of our body.

anger issues and an eating disorder. For 67 years he has struggled with the fallout of his father's failure as a parent.

Another friend's brother was murdered. My friend was sure that his sister-in-law had killed her husband. How does he separate his bitter anger at her from his need to grieve for his brother?

The first challenge is for my friends to be able to forgive the offender, it is not optional if they are going to heal. The second challenge is for those who desire to minister to either of them. We must minister to the anger as well as the grief. Both of them were grievously harmed, by man's standards they have every right to be angry. How do we speak to their anger? Only the Holy Spirit can give us the wisdom necessary to speak the right words at the right time.

Chapter 2

A Life Divided

Most of us alive at the time of John F. Kennedy's assassination can tell you exactly where we were at the time we heard the news. We remember the sights of those days: the airplane bearing the President's body, the caisson carrying the body through the streets of Washington D.C. on its way to Arlington. We remember Jacqueline, John Boy and Caroline stoically watching the events unfold. We remember Walter Cronkite, Chet Huntley and David Brinkley solemnly reporting the dreadful news, all in the starkness of black and white television. It has been 53 years since I watched those days unfold and I still remember where I was when I heard of his death and I can take you back to that spot, in a school bus outside the Central School on Michigan Street.

Others will remember the disintegration of the shuttle Challenger shortly after it lifted off into the sky while being filmed in vivid color. We remember the euphoria leading up to the launch as we celebrated the first school teacher, the first 'one of us', to lift off into space and we remember the explosion that followed.

We remember President Reagan commemorating the lives of these astronauts saying, *"We will never forget them, nor the last time we saw them, this morning, as they prepared for their journey and waved goodbye and "slipped the surly bonds of earth" to "touch the face of God.""*

We think of the events of 9/11, a day instantly recognized by two numbers identifying the month and the day, the year, 2001, being unnecessary. We remember being glued to the television set or computer monitor as the images of the airplanes slicing into the towers became forever etched in our memory. We can tell you where we were, who we were with, what we felt and how life just stopped for a few days as we tried to process the heartache, the grief, the unknowing where this new manifestation of evil would lead.

In the same way, those who have experienced the death of a dear loved one have the memory of those horrific minutes, hours and days forever seared into their memory banks and can recall with detail where they were, who they were with and their emotions as the final breath of their loved one slipped away. When we use a GPS to drive to a new location and miss a turn, the kind lady who has been giving us directions says, "Recalibrating" and then proceeds to supply us with instructions as to how to arrive at our destination. Our lives are like that when we have been dealt a devastating blow, one that threatens to divide our life. For a period of time our mind and heart are 'recalibrating', trying to assimilate all of this new information and begin to make some sense of it all before proceeding.

The mother who sat beside the bed of her young son, holding his hand and stroking his forehead will never in this lifetime forget the sights, the sounds or the emotions of those last few hours. The father who was driving the night the drunken driver smashed into their car, taking the life of his only daughter will never forget. Years later they both will be able to recount in vivid detail, more detail than they would like, the trauma that forever changed their life.

Some of life's experiences are life-changing such as the death of a child, the death of our only love, the death of the parent who believed in us when no one else would. These divide our life into 'pre' and 'post'; before and after.   These events cannot be walked around. They can only be walked through like a tornado-torn street with uprooted trees, hanging wires, nail-laden shingles and household items from a family home two miles away. We can never take this path unchanged. From the perspective of the believer we will either be drawn to God or pushed away. Our faith will be increased or it will become almost not-existent. We will sing a new song or we will go through the motions of the old. We will be His ambassador, living out a Job-like, halting, stammering trust or we will walk away in seething silence.

For some it may change life negatively: the death of a parent that results in a life of promiscuity; the trauma of a bankruptcy that results in eventual suicide; the horrors of the battlefield that lead to PTSD. For others those same events may result in a life's walk through the valley of the shadow hand in hand with the Good Shepherd.

And for those of us looking on, can we understand those who still struggle with the grief so many years after its cause? Maybe you have known someone who has experienced one of those life-altering events. How do you react to them? How do you minister to them? How do you judge them? If someone were to ask one of them about your ministry to them in their time of need what would they say about you?

We recount the events of our national tragedies and wonder 'what if?' What if someone would have paid more attention to Lee Harvey Oswald, or the seals on the shuttle or the men who only cared about flying planes but were not interested in how to land them? What if we would have taken our son to the doctor sooner and not dismissed his complaints as just part of being a growing boy? What if we had taken another route home, a route not shared with a drunken driver?

A Scottish preacher in the last century who had lost his wife delivered an unusually personal sermon just after her death. In the message, he admitted that he did not understand this life. But still less could he understand how people facing loss could abandon the faith. "Abandon it for what!" he cried. "You people in the sunshine may believe the faith, but we in the shadow must believe it. We have nothing else."

Permission to Grieve

The Bible gives us permission to grieve. The scriptures are full of examples of God's chosen people who have shown their grief publicly and He has written their words down for us to read and to learn from.

Jesus wept, Paul sorrowed, the Psalmists lamented, Job grieved, Habakkuk cried out and the prophets expressed the burden of Israel's sin. The Apostle Paul seemed conflicted however. He wrote In Philippians that we are to *"rejoice in the Lord always."* [5]

---

5 Philippians 4:4 Rejoice in the Lord always, and again I say rejoice

When he wrote to the same group of people about Epaphroditus' being close to death he said God's mercy in healing Epaphroditus prevented Paul from having *"sorrow upon sorrow."*[6] On one hand he said that we should always rejoice and on the other hand he said the death of his friend would cause sorrow on top of sorrow. We will see examples of this at work in the life of certain believers as we proceed through the study.

I have known church leaders who feel it would set a bad example if they show grief, believing that they must maintain their spiritual facade no matter how difficult their loss. Whether we are rejoicing or sorrowful there is a standard for our life.

> *1 Corinthians 4:7-11 But we have this treasure in earthen vessels, that the excellency of the power may be of God, and not of us. We are troubled on every side, yet not distressed; we are perplexed, but not in despair; Persecuted, but not forsaken; cast down, but not destroyed; always bearing about in the body the dying of the Lord Jesus, that the life also of Jesus might be made manifest in our body. For we which live are always delivered unto death for Jesus' sake, that the life also of Jesus might be made manifest in our mortal flesh.*

It is not wrong to show grief, but it is wrong to let it define our life. It is not wrong to not rejoice for a period of time but it is wrong to forget how to rejoice in the Lord.

---

6 Philippians 2:25-27 Yet I supposed it necessary to send to you Epaphroditus, my brother, and companion in labour, and fellowsoldier, but your messenger, and he that ministered to my wants. For he longed after you all, and was full of heaviness, because that ye had heard that he had been sick. For indeed he was sick nigh unto death: but God had mercy on him; and not on him only, but on me also, lest I should have sorrow upon sorrow.

To those who are in need Jesus reaches down and says, *"Come unto me, all ye that labour and are heavy laden, and I will give you rest. Take my yoke upon you, and learn of me; for I am meek and lowly in heart: and ye shall find rest unto your souls. For my yoke is easy, and my burden is light."*[7]

We are to be the ones who make the life of Jesus evident in our mortal flesh. We are the ones who 'are the only Jesus that some will ever see.' Losing a dear loved one does not let us off the hook for carrying His image to a lost and dying world.

A Special Problem

It is one of my observations that many times men have a much more difficult time expressing their grief than do women. Men historically in culture are the protectors and at a significant time of loss or death it is a reminder to them that they have failed to fulfill their role. At times when they seem cold or disinterested it may be that they are struggling at a whole different level than it appears on the surface. I have had men leave my office and sit in their car while their wife or daughter made the arrangements for a burial. I have had women come to my office alone to pick out a cemetery plot and a marker for their own pending death—their husband could not bear the thought of being there.

It is easy to mock them or to be angry with them but until we begin to listen to their heart, if we can get close enough to them for them to express it, we will never know the pain they are experiencing.

Churches have historically taught that husbands and fathers are to be the head of the home, that

---

7   Matthew 11:28-30

they are responsible for the stability, safety and godliness of the home and they back that up from the Word of God. It is understandable then that these same husbands and fathers feel they have failed when something as grievous as death invades their family.

> Psalm 94:17–19 Unless the Lord had been my help, My soul had almost dwelt in silence. When I said, My foot slippeth; Thy mercy, O Lord, held me up. In the multitude of my thoughts within me Thy comforts delight my soul.

How does the strong husband grieve? He can't weep, not in front of his wife and children anyway. If he is a godly man he can't punch a hole through the wall. He can't go to a bar and drown his sorrows. He usually does not have a friend he can discuss his weakness with. He is left to bear the pain stoically.

Husbands and wives have sat two feet apart in my office and hurled accusations at each other because they cannot understand the way the other is expressing their grief. He is angry because all she does is cry. She is angry at her loss, at the fact that he doesn't seem to be showing any grief at all, and because she feels she has to grieve for them both. He is angry with her because her non-stop tears are just another reminder that he has failed. He needs her to 'man up' and move on with her life and let him off the hook just a little. She wants him to express his grief the way she does.

Grief Delayed

A counselor friend told me that grief denied is only grief delayed. It isn't a matter of 'if' we will grieve, it is a matter of 'when.' And grief delayed may express itself in ways that will be difficult to understand years after the trial.

The mother of a friend in her 40s died. Making the death more difficult is the fact that her brother is mentally ill. He wants to make decisions regarding the burial but does not have the mental ability to fully participate in the decisions or the cost of those decisions. Our friend has not been able to grieve for her mother because her time is spent worrying about and caring for her mentally ill brother. One day she was his sister and the next day she took on the role of his mother, all without being able to have time for her own grief. She asked, "when will I be able to grieve?"

Some may deny grief because they don't want to feel weak. Some may have seen someone carry on in their grief in an effort to draw attention to themselves and do not want to emulate that example. Some may have known someone who seemed never to get over a trial in their life and do not want to live the rest of their life like that—so they choose to try not to grieve at all.

Chapter 3

The Answer for the Pain of Grief

Knowing the answer of how to deal with the anguish of grief does not earn an "A" on the test. It is how we live out the answer in our daily life which shows those watching that God is enough for life's every trial. There is a difference between knowing the correct answers about how to live when life hurts and actually living those answers in the difficult days and dark nights of our grief.

When Will I Find Closure?

Someone said, *"Closure is a term we should not use because we do not 'close out' our grieving but our lives move on...changed."* The loss that has caused our grief is not a former part of our life that has passed but is a chapter in an ongoing book. It is a chapter that changes us in the same way a marriage or a child's birth has a continuing effect on our life's story.

What does grief look like? How long should the grieving 'process' last? When will life get back to 'normal' again? These are all questions that are only natural to ask and it is reasonable to expect a helpful answer. The problem is that there is no answer to any of those questions.

> Jesus Christ is no security against storms, but He is perfect security in storms. He has never promised you an easy passage, only a safe landing. Unknown

Many of us speak of the 'grieving process.' The word 'process' makes it sound as though somewhere there is a list of items that one methodically goes through, checking off one after the other until the 'process' is finalized. The word makes it sound as though there is an end that can be reached after which life returns to 'normal.'

> Ed received a call from the western college that his son attended informing him that his son had not shown up for classes and they were concerned about him. He was a healthy young man, an avid skier and outdoorsman. He was the apple of his father's eye and the sole heir to carry on the family name. But when they went to his apartment they found him dead of natural causes. Ed's wife died that day as well—not physically but emotionally.

> Many times when talking to someone in the throes of grief you can see signs of encouragement that someday they are going to see the daylight again. But it is not so with his wife. There is no glimmer of pending health. When I talk to Ed he says, "I just want life to get back to normal again." It is left to me to be the bearer of bad news; that the old 'normal' died in the

apartment with his son and is buried in the same grave. There is no going back. There is no 'process' that can take this family back to the days when their son was alive—back to the days when life was 'normal.'

Why do we think the death of a significant part or our identity will not change us permanently? Why do we think life will somehow return to 'normal' when the normal we previously knew can never return? We will have a different normal but the previous one is gone. It is our choice how that new normal will evidence itself in our life from this point forward.

We can respond to trials in differing ways. One is that we begin to take on the trial as 'just the way life is.' We just accept the difficulty as our new lifestyle. We may not enjoy the trial but we are resigned to it and believe that this will define our lives from this time forward.

The other response is that we just want out of the trial no matter what the cost. I think of two people who lost their spouses to divorce who insisted on getting remarried when it was clearly not in anyone's best interest to do so that soon. They wanted a spouse more than they wanted to grow in the Lord; more than they wanted to learn from their trial and more than they wanted to look like Jesus.

Should Christians Grieve Differently than Non-Christians?

Ed's story about the death of his son reminds us that once the journey down this new path is started you may stop or proceed but there is no option to go back. Death has a way of dashing to smithereens the best that we have—hope.

*1 Thessalonians 4:13 But I would not have you
to be ignorant, brethren, concerning them which
are asleep, that ye sorrow not, even as others
which have no hope.*

Paul is not saying in this passage that Christians
are not to grieve but he is stating emphatically
that Christians should grieve differently than non-
Christians. The reason? Hope. It is more than the
fact that we are going to see our loved ones again; it
is that we are going to share perfect fellowship with
them around the throne of God. It is that we will
never be separated again, it is that no one that we
know or love will ever suffer death or even a runny
nose again. But mainly it is that our relationship and
our fellowship will be perfect, centered around the
basis for our hope—Jesus Christ.

One of my favorite scriptures is the angel's
pronouncement to the shepherds, *"And the angel said
unto them, Fear not: for, behold, I bring you good tidings of
great joy, which shall be to all people. For unto you is born
this day in the city of David a Saviour, which is Christ the
Lord."* [8] That pronouncement changed for all time the
Believer's outlook on life and on death. We usually
limit those words to the birth of the Baby on that first
Christmas but they were intended as much for us
today as for them two millennia ago.

The shepherds who heard the heralded
announcement of peace, good tidings and great joy
and who traveled to see the Christ child that evening
woke up the next morning in a world where disease
was still rampant; Roman soldiers still mistreated
the weak, crops continued to fail in drought, wives
miscarried, children went prodigal, loved ones died
and sin and sinners were evident throughout the land.

---

8   Luke 2:10-11

The angel's announcement signaled the end of all of that—death and evil are temporarily still with us but their power has been broken forever and someday they will cease to exist for the Believer. We have a sure hope, promised to us by God Himself. Our hope is not just for that future time when we will be free from pain and death but Jesus Christ is the Living Hope[9] for today—even in our grief.

Psalm 36:5-10 Thy mercy, O Lord, is in the heavens; and thy faithfulness reacheth unto the clouds. Thy righteousness is like the great mountains; thy judgments are a great deep: O Lord, thou preservest man and beast. How excellent is thy lovingkindness, O God! therefore the children of men put their trust under the shadow of thy wings. They shall be abundantly satisfied with the fatness of thy house; and thou shalt make them drink of the river of thy pleasures. For with thee is the fountain of life: in thy light shall we see light. O continue thy lovingkindness unto them that know thee; and thy righteousness to the upright in heart.

Theologians speak about the "already but not yet." We have the Lord's sure promise of peace but have only a foretaste now. The day is coming when we will live forever in total fulfillment of the promise of perfect peace. We are living in the "not yet" part of the "already." God's promise of healing has been made, the die is cast, it cannot be changed by mankind nor by Satan and his demons even though we still face disease, death and heartache. *"Fear not! I bring you good tidings of great joy."* And God always keeps His promises.

---

9 1 Peter 1:3 Blessed be the God and Father of our Lord Jesus Christ, which according to his abundant mercy hath begotten us again unto a lively hope by the resurrection of Jesus Christ from the dead,

Change Is Good—Even When It Seems To Be Bad

The status-quo often seems better and safer to us than the unknown. God never seems to be satisfied in leaving us there however. No one looks forward to trials as a means of growth but the Lord uses them many times to fashion us in His image.

> *James 1:2-4 My brethren, count it all joy when ye fall into divers temptations; Knowing this, that the trying of your faith worketh patience. But let patience have her perfect work, that ye may be perfect and entire, wanting nothing.*

James is not proposing that we *"count it all joy"* because our spouse died or because we have been diagnosed with a terminal disease. He is telling us that when our faith is tested and we look to *"the Father of lights, with whom is no variableness, neither shadow of turning"* [10] that we will grow in our faith, trust and knowledge of Him—and that is always good.

We, as Christians, should never be satisfied where we are in our spiritual walk. If the apostle Paul was not far enough along in his walk to be satisfied we should not be satisfied with our walk either.

> *Philippians 3:13-14 Brethren, I count not myself to have apprehended: but this one thing I do, forgetting those things which are behind, and reaching forth unto those things which are before, I press toward the mark for the prize of the high calling of God in Christ Jesus.*

God intends for our new normal to be better than our old normal. He desires that our new normal look more like Him than did our life before our loss.

---

10   James 1:17   Every good gift and every perfect gift is from above, and cometh down from the Father of lights, with whom is no variableness, neither shadow of turning.

How Do You Want People to Respond to Your Grief?

We do not all grieve alike and it is unfair for us to try to force anyone into a box or set pattern as to how to grieve. When we are grieving, however, we must also allow others to minister to us in different ways and use different methods than we might choose. Our heart is broken, our nerves are frayed and our emotions are raw. It is very difficult for someone to know how to minister to us at any given moment. There are seven accepted stages of grief that we move back and forth through. We may have been in "shock and denial" yesterday but be in "anger and bargaining" today and in "Depression, Reflection and Loneliness" tomorrow.[11]

> It is amazing how the Lord works in so many lives and on so many levels. It is almost like He is smarter than us, but from my prayers advising Him on how He should respond to what I ask for we know that is not true. (Said tongue-in-cheek) KC

Many people who want to offer comfort don't know what to say to someone overwhelmed by grief. They don't want to say something silly or insulting so they either say nothing at all or try to say something 'safe.' People are afraid to say something that will tear open the wound again.

A friend of mine whose 20 year-old daughter was killed in a tragic automobile accident said that he and his wife love it when people mention their daughter. I asked him if those sending his family Christmas cards

---

11 See Appendix for the Stages of Grief. They are out of order for my illustration here. The Stages of Grief are not set in stone as the 'process' in which everyone will grieve but are a generally observed pattern.

should mention his daughter's name, even ten years after her death. He said it was not the responsibility of their friends and church family to do their family's grieving for them, that was their job. He said that to receive a card calling them to a "Merry Christmas" was a reminder to the family that the Gospel was good news—even to those whose daughter was killed in a tragic accident. He was accepting the ministry as given and not placing demands on those who were clearly trying to comfort his family at a very difficult time.

I met with the wife of a friend who had passed away rather unexpectedly only the day before. She told me about finding her husband of 46 years in his favorite chair that morning where he had passed away peacefully. In my effort to comfort her I almost started to say, "I know how you feel" when I caught myself. I admitted to her that I had no idea how she felt but that I felt very badly for the loss she had just experienced and the lonely days ahead. She replied by saying, "I was thinking this morning that I have said some awfully silly things to people when I didn't have a clue how badly they were hurting. Why did I do that?" She understood my poor selection of words because she could sense my heart was sincere. My poor choice of words spoken from a heart of compassion were better than showing no compassion at all.

Looking for Help With Our Grief

There is an old country song that says, "Looking for love in all the wrong places." It is not only applicable to romantic love but it is applicable to the entire scope of our life when we look for love, for affirmation, for comfort, for the fulfillment of our dream, for our hope, in any place other than Jesus Christ.

We may desire to have our grief assuaged by other people. Some men and women whose spouse has died seek to fill the hole by remarrying as quickly as possible. Some forego marriage and just move in together. A friend of mine, in his early 80s, couldn't function alone after his wife died and moved in with a single lady in her late 70s. This was not an acceptable societal practice for him as a young man but as an older man, in his grief, he found it better than being alone. He said to me, "I know that I am living in sin but I need someone to be with."

Some may look to comfort their grief in alcohol or drugs whether legal or illegal. Some seek to replace the lost intimacy with illegitimate sex. Some spend money wildly, hoping to fill the hole in their heart with things.

Understanding that our Father-child relationship with God is unchangeable is essential in the hard times. I asked a friend how he and his wife managed to hold their lives together after the death of their daughter when other families who have faced the death of a child had been unable to do so. He said that his strength after her death was contingent on what he knew about God before her death. He told those who had gathered near the Emergency Room the day of her death that "God is still on His throne." He knew that to be a true statement, he also knew that he would see his daughter again someday. He knew that God could sustain him through his grief. His progression towards healing has not been based on his feelings but on his knowledge. He still tears up almost ten years after her death but he goes back to what he knows to be true—God is still on His throne.

Psalm 32:10-11 Many sorrows shall be to the wicked: but he that trusteth in the LORD, mercy shall compass him about. Be glad in the LORD, and rejoice, ye righteous: and shout for joy, all ye that are upright in heart.

Seeking Help from Above

If you need help in your time of grief it is essential that you be cautious as to where you seek that help. It is not necessary to find someone who has suffered the exact same loss that you have but it is important for a mature Christian to help you. Be careful about seeking help from someone of the opposite sex because it is far too easy to develop an emotional affair that has great potential ultimately to add to your grief. Seek out someone who is more mature than you are rather than someone who is at the same point in their journey as yourself. Be careful about expecting anyone, even the most mature of Christians, to fill the void in your life that only God should and can fill.

> *Psalm 121:1-2 I will lift up mine eyes unto the hills, from whence cometh my help. My help cometh from the Lord, which made heaven and earth.*

> *Deuteronomy 33:27 The eternal God is thy refuge, and underneath are the everlasting arms: and he shall thrust out the enemy from before thee; and shall say, Destroy them.*

> *Isaiah 26:3-4 Thou wilt keep him in perfect peace, whose mind is stayed on thee: because he trusteth in thee. Trust ye in the LORD for ever: for in the LORD JEHOVAH is everlasting strength:*

> *Isaiah 26:8-9 Yea, in the way of thy judgments, O LORD, have we waited for thee; the desire of our soul is to thy name, and to the remembrance of thee. With my soul have I desired thee in the night; yea, with my spirit within me will I seek thee early: for when thy judgments are in the*

earth, the inhabitants of the world will learn righteousness.

Psalm 142:3-6 When my spirit was overwhelmed within me, then thou knewest my path. In the way wherein I walked have they privily laid a snare for me. I looked on my right hand, and beheld, but there was no man that would know me: refuge failed me; no man cared for my soul. I cried unto thee, O LORD: I said, Thou art my refuge and my portion in the land of the living. Attend unto my cry; for I am brought very low: deliver me from my persecutors; for they are stronger than I.

Do You Want to Be Well?

Maybe we are unable to heal from our grief because we do not want to be healed. Pastor Jon M. Jenkin's sermons[12] on the man at the pool of Bethesda[13] included the thought that because the man had been there for 38 years he had made himself as comfortable as possible. He may have found a bed to lie on and he might have installed some shelving with a vase of flowers and a few knick-knacks. The point was that sometimes we find a comfort level in our grief that begins to identify us.

My wife and I went through a series of God-appointed trials that all ran together for a period of about 20 years. At the end of that time as I began to heal and life began to find a new normal I was concerned that I was again about to make a change towards a life that was strange and unknown to me—and I was afraid. For many years I had been

---

12   Title of the sermon series is "Thriving or Surviving"

13   John 5:6 When Jesus saw him lie, and knew that he had been now a long time in that case, he saith unto him, Wilt thou be made whole?

identifying myself as "Karl...the broken one." God wanted to identify me as "Karl...the mended one" and I was more secure in my brokenness than in the unknown of being mended. By my fear I was loudly stating that God was not enough.

There are truths that we can learn from this miracle at the pool of Bethesda that will help us in healing from our grief.

◊ Be the one in the multitude that Jesus sees as "miracle ready." There were many people there that day but Scripture only records one being healed. In man's eyes, he was the least likely but he was in the place to show God's glory and power to the greatest extent.

◊ The question *"wilt thou be made whole"* is open ended. It is, "are you all in?" It is, "will you do whatever I ask?" Even if it is to dip 7 times in a muddy river to heal your leprosy? [14] Even if it is to let Him use spit and mud on your eyes to heal them? [15] Even if it is to humble you and to test you in some other way?

When my wife and I were going through those black years I read the Bible, I read good books on what I felt my needs were, I tried to pray as best I

---

14   2 Kings 5:14 Then went he down, and dipped himself seven times in Jordan, according to the saying of the man of God: and his flesh came again like unto the flesh of a little child, and he was clean.

15   John 9:6-7 When he had thus spoken, he spat on the ground, and made clay of the spittle, and he anointed the eyes of the blind man with the clay, And said unto him, Go, wash in the pool of Siloam, (which is by interpretation, Sent.) He went his way therefore, and washed, and came seeing.

could, I journaled my thoughts and I drove her nuts talking about it. I did that because I did not want to waste the trial. I was hurting so much that I did not want the Lord to have to take me back through the trial in order to reteach me all or part of it. Trials are to help us on our journey of looking more like Jesus. God wants to meet us in our grief. He is both resolute and patient. He will give us time to grow in him but He will continue to take us through the trial in increasing intensity to achieve His purposes.

Do we want to be healed? Do we want to begin a new phase of our life, another 'new normal?' Or are we satisfied with being here, in our grief, for the rest of our life?

Should We All Grieve Alike?

Our lives are a living testimony service. We are constantly living 'like' or 'unlike' Jesus and our grieving is no exception. Does this mean that we are all to grieve in some sterile manner, exactly like the person sitting on the other side of the church or to not grieve at all? Absolutely not! Thinking back through the saints of the Old and New Testaments we see a wide range of personality types. Some were bold while others were more sensitive. Some took charge while others stayed more in the background. Even though the Holy Spirit authored God's Word using various men we see their differing personalities coming through their writings. We too have differing personalities and more than likely will grieve differently. Even siblings grieve in vastly differing ways. God allows each of us to grieve differently as long as we grieve in a manner honoring to Him.

Some of you have had both parents die at this point in your life as have I. You and I may grieve differently because we had different relationships with our parents yet we can still both look like Jesus. Some have close-knit families and grieve the loss of that closeness. Others have families that maintained a certain distance or aloofness between members and when the parents die the hope for closeness dies as well.

> Life must go on, I forget just why.
>
> Edna St. Vincent Millay

Sometimes we come to the point where the above words ring true for us. But the gracious Father gives our life purpose and meaning—even in the darkest times.

One man whose wife died in 1970, visited her grave every single day throughout the summer and winter. When he could no longer drive into the cemetery because of the snow he would park across the road from the cemetery and walk through the knee-deep snow to her grave. Later he began going to Florida in the winter but every day he was in town he visited her grave until he died in 2005. Was he wrong to continue this practice, was he not getting over his grief? I talked with him a number of times and believe it was not grief that caused him to go to the cemetery every day as much as it was that he was honoring the love he had for his wife.

One man visits the grave every day for 35 years; one daughter throws her body across her mother's casket; one wife lays prostrate on her husband's grave; others walk stoically away from the casket which holds the remains of a dear loved one. Some graveside services are family reunions with hugs and laughter while others are somber events with tears and lots of Kleenex. Which one is right and which one is wrong? Without walking with those people for a time we cannot know the answer.

Grief is not a process:

◊ In that it has an end where it no longer exists. That grief should not cripple us but it should change us. It should grow us in the image of God, not cause us to be angry, bitter or drive us 'inside' ourselves.

◊ In that it has a methodology. There is not one manner in which to heal but there is one Man, Christ Jesus, whom our grief must pass through. My road may be different than yours but it will lead to and through the same place— Jesus Christ.

◊ In that it has mile markers that can be checked off one after the other. It requires prayer, patience and the reminder that God has a plan for this. Some will move through quickly, some slowly and some may need to take the class over again.

Hope Shining Through Grief

First Peter 3:15 says the child of God should stand ever ready to give an answer for *"the hope that is in you."*[16] How we grieve is one of those ways in which we demonstrate our hope to a lost world that has none.

God does not leave us hopeless nor does He leave us helpless. Rather than saying, "I will do it myself" we should say, *"I can do all things through Christ which strengtheneth me."*[17] God is not saying to us, "here is

---

16 1 Peter 3:15 But sanctify the Lord God in your hearts: and be ready always to give an answer to every man that asketh you a reason of the hope that is in you with meekness and fear:

17 Philippians 4:13

how you have to grieve," He is saying to each one of us who are hurting, "let Me help."

> *Psalm 40:1-3 To the chief Musician, A Psalm of David. I waited patiently for the LORD; and he inclined unto me, and heard my cry. He brought me up also out of an horrible pit, out of the miry clay, and set my feet upon a rock, and established my goings. And he hath put a new song in my mouth, even praise unto our God: many shall see it, and fear, and shall trust in the LORD.*

One believer may face the death of a parent, another faces the death of a spouse and yet another experiences the death of a child. All of them face the death of someone they love but each loss is entirely different. One believer may face the death of a parent who loved them, cared for them and supported them throughout their life while another faces the death of the parent that abused them physically and emotionally during their childhood years and could never find a kind word to say for them as adults. Both face the death of a parent but each has a completely different time of testing to walk through.

We may think that the woman whose abusive, alcoholic husband died after 40 years of a troubled marriage would not grieve. We may think that there would be such a sigh of relief and that she would dance a jig. She may grieve very deeply however. She may grieve that her hope has died. She may grieve that the hope that someday he would be the husband he promised to be at their wedding ceremony has died. She may grieve that the hope that someday he would be the father to their three children that he should have been and the hope that he would apologize for the missed sports activities, school plays and mental abuse has died. She may grieve the wasted years;

she was an attractive 20 year-old young girl in a white gown back then, now she is a haggard 60 year-old in jeans and a sweatshirt that she wears to her job in the factory.

She may grieve his lasting influence on their children, wishing she had risked the difficult life of single motherhood to protect them. She may grieve that, after paying for the funeral, she is left with no savings, an apartment in a poor part of town and no retirement account. She may grieve what she imagines the rest of her life to be as she hates the thought of having to work into her 70s even though her health is not good. She may grieve the unknown, imagining it to be even worse than her life up to now.

> God ordains the direction of our life; He also ordains the disruptions in our life.
>
> Dr. Jon M. Jenkins

She may grieve for the young man that she had loved and married but who died a broken man, never achieving the dreams they had spoken so often of when they were dating. She has much to grieve, she has lost far more than any of us can imagine.

For any of us to say 'because you have faced the death of a loved one here is how you must respond' is hurtful and wrong. We must be careful to honor the Lord in our grieving and in how we minister His comfort to those who are in the throes of grief.

Psalm 3:2 Many there be which say of my soul, There is no help for him in God. Selah. But thou, O Lord, art a shield for me; my glory, and the lifter up of mine head. I cried unto the Lord with my voice, and he heard me out of his holy hill. Selah. I laid me down and slept; I awaked; for the Lord sustained me.

Chapter 4

The Necessity of Prayer

For the grieving Christian there is no substitute for prayer.[18] It is difficult to imagine any type of relationship being successful if one party refuses to speak. It is my nature to 'clam up' when I am hurting emotionally. There are many reasons for this I am sure but the one that I like the best is that 'I am quiet because I am processing.' And while there may be other reasons for my quietness, it is a fact that is the way I work through a problem.

If you were to ask my wife about the nobleness of my 'processing' she would give you a different answer and tell you that just the time when she needs me to talk I have gone somewhere inside myself. She would tell you that I might not 'come out' for days or weeks. The way she tells it is not nearly as noble as the way I present it. Because of her personality she needs to talk while my personality pushes me to quietness.

---

18   There is no substitute for prayer for the Christian who is not grieving either. Prayer is to be a natural part of our Christian daily life.

49

Another problem with processing internally is that sometimes we don't communicate with the Lord either. We 'clam up' with Him as well. There may be many reasons why the Lord doesn't answer our prayers the way that we want Him to but it is impossible for God to answer prayers that we do not pray. *You have not because you ask not."* [19]

The Scriptures assume that there will be an ongoing dialogue between Father and child; between God and man. As dysfunctional as our marriage is when I stop talking to my wife so is my fellowship with God dysfunctional when I stop talking to Him.

> When pondering the mysteries of life, hold on to what you know for sure and never doubt in the darkness what god has taught you in the light.
>
> Warren Wiersbe

But Why Pray?

My wife and I travel 45 minutes each way to church and many times I use that time to ask her opinion about various spiritual topics or scriptures I am thinking through. She is my favorite person to discuss these things with because she knows the Word and is committed to obeying it. Talking with her always makes me better.

On a much grander scale, talking with God makes me even better yet. Talking with Him bends me towards holiness. When I open my heart to Him and express my thoughts I hear them in a new way. Sometimes I sound broken, other times I sound demanding or petty. When I let the Holy Spirit take my thoughts and my words He convicts me or encourages me.

---

19   James 4:3

Why pray? Because the Bible says we are to *"pray without ceasing."* 1 Thessalonians 5:17

Why pray? Because Jesus, our Example, did. *"And it came to pass in those days, that he went out into a mountain to pray, and continued all night in prayer to God."* Luke 6:12

Why pray? Because God hears. *"In my distress I called upon the LORD, and cried to my God: and he did hear my voice out of his temple, and my cry did enter into his ears."* 1 Samuel 22:7

Why pray? Because prayer works. *"The effectual fervent prayer of a righteous man availeth much."* James 5:16

God may answer, "No", meaning that what we have now is better for us than the change we hope and pray for. He may answer, "Not now", because what we are asking for will be better for us in the future than now. He may answer, "Not at all", because He has something better for us. Why pray? Because our loving heavenly Father asks us to. He desires that we express to Him our heart and mind in trust and in praise.

Even If The Answer Is No

Prayer speaks to our dependence; to our acknowledgement that He is God and it speaks to the stick-to-it-iveness of our heart. Prayer is the other half of our conversation with God. Scripture reading is the half where God shares His heart with us and prayer is the half where we share our heart with Him.

I asked my wife on one those trips to church why we would bother to pray if God already knows what we are going for to pray and how He will answer. After we had discussed this for quite a few minutes she said, "we pray for what we hope for with a heart that is contented—even if the answer is no."

Her answer has stuck with me since that time. Can I be contented with God's answer to my prayer even if His answer is "no"? Am I contented with His answer even if He says no to physical healing? Even if He says no to a new job? Even if He says no to relief from the storm?

There are scriptural examples of praying for a desired outcome only to have the Lord respond differently than had been hoped.

◊ Jesus prayed for the cup to be removed only to walk with a contented heart to the cross. His physical body was broken but His heart was at peace with His Father until His final cry. God's answer was no—this is part of My plan.

◊ Paul prayed for the thorn to be removed only to 'glory in his infirmity' if that infirmity was used to glorify God.[20] God's answer was no—this way is best.

◊ Abraham and Sarah tried to hurry up God's promise of a child. God's answer was no—not now, not this way.

---

20 2 Corinthians 12:7-10 And lest I should be exalted above measure through the abundance of the revelations, there was given to me a thorn in the flesh, the messenger of Satan to buffet me, lest I should be exalted above measure. For this thing I besought the Lord thrice, that it might depart from me. And he said unto me, My grace is sufficient for thee: for my strength is made perfect in weakness. Most gladly therefore will I rather glory in my infirmities, that the power of Christ may rest upon me. Therefore I take pleasure in infirmities, in reproaches, in necessities, in persecutions, in distresses for Christ's sake: for when I am weak, then am I strong.

In the Garden of Gethsemane Jesus prayed, *"O my Father, if it be possible, let this cup pass from me:"*[21] Dare we question Jesus' faith? Dare we question His holiness? Yet we know that this prayer was not answered in the way He asked it would be. It was necessary for Jesus to go to the cross. Jesus follows up His prayer request with, *"nevertheless not as I will, but as thou wilt"* which is a better way of saying "even if the answer is no."

The Apostle Paul suffered with a *"thorn in the flesh."* It is unnecessary to know what the thorn was but we see that Paul felt that it hindered his ministry and he thought that it only made sense that it be removed. He prayed three times for its removal but was more than satisfied "even if the answer was no." Paul was thankful for his weakness that caused Christ's power to rest upon him. We all want our trials to be removed so we can be strong again.

God Desires to Give Us What is Best for Us

In the eleventh chapter of the book of Numbers, there is a story of God's people grumbling about the manna that God had provided for them. They cried out to Moses and to God to give them meat to eat. God heard their cries and answered their prayer, but what they wanted; what they received, was not a blessing after all.

> *Psalm 106:15 And he gave them their request; but sent leanness into their soul.*

There may be times when we want something so badly and pray for it for so long that God sends us what we want and along with the answer we receive leanness into our soul. Often we are sure that we

---

21   Matthew 26:39

know better what is good for us than God does. And every time we think that way, we are wrong. Isn't it better to pray as Jesus did, *"nevertheless not as I will, but as thou wilt"*?

> We say 'Jesus is all I need'. But we will never know Jesus is all we need until Jesus is all we have, then we will know that Jesus is all we need.
>
> Vance Havner.

While Jesus certainly taught perseverance in prayer[22] He also set the example for us of praying three times followed by accepting God's will. Paul followed that example when he prayed for removal of the thorn in the flesh. Years ago I was troubled about an issue and prayed for the Lord to resolve it. I no longer remember the issue I was praying about but I remember praying passionately about it one morning and the Lord stopping me. I knew at that time I was not to pray about it again and I didn't. To this day I am not sure why God stopped me but I know just as sure as the Apostle Paul did that I was no longer to pray about it. It taught me that I need to be sensitive to the Holy Spirit's leading as I pray.

> *Romans 11:33 O the depth of the riches both of the wisdom and knowledge of God! how unsearchable are his judgments, and his ways past finding out!*

How to pray

Fervently—

James 5:16 Confess your faults one to another, and pray one for another, that ye may be healed. The effectual fervent prayer of a righteous man availeth much.

---

22   Luke 18:1-9 The Parable of the Unjust Judge

54

Continually—

1 Thessalonians 5:17 Pray without ceasing.

Luke 18:1 And he spake a parable unto them to this end, that men ought always to pray, and not to faint;

Submissively—

Romans 8:26-27 Likewise the Spirit also helpeth our infirmities: for we know not what we should pray for as we ought: but the Spirit itself maketh intercession for us with groanings which cannot be uttered. And he that searcheth the hearts knoweth what is the mind of the Spirit, because he maketh intercession for the saints according to the will of God.

Expectantly with a listening ear—

1 Kings 19:11-12 And he said, Go forth, and stand upon the mount before the LORD. And, behold, the LORD passed by, and a great and strong wind rent the mountains, and brake in pieces the rocks before the LORD; but the LORD was not in the wind: and after the wind an earthquake; but the LORD was not in the earthquake: And after the earthquake a fire; but the LORD was not in the fire: and after the fire a still small voice.

In holiness—

Psalm 66:18 If I regard iniquity in my heart, the Lord will not hear me:

In What Ways do We Choose to Listen to God Poorly?

A Facebook post by Grammarly said *"The biggest communication problem is that we do not listen to understand, we listen to reply."* That is a truth for many of us as we converse with a friend. We listen only long enough to be able to respond with our argument rather than listening in order to learn or to hear their heart. Many times we listen to God the same way, we tell Him what we want without listening to His voice or to His heart.

We listen poorly when:

◊ We want some grandiose answer from the whirlwind, not the still small voice.

◊ We do not search Scripture.

◊ We do not listen to the wise, godly counsel of others.

◊ We will not listen to God's answer if it doesn't precisely answer the question we asked.

◊ We ask in prayer and then move on to something or someone else before God answers.

◊ We answer our question for Him. We presume to know how God will, or should, answer, and proceed without waiting

◊ We hold on to our sins, refusing to confess them.

◊ We do not listen in faith, we demand sight.

Ways That God Speaks

Through the still small voice—

1 Kings 19:11-12 And he said, Go forth, and stand upon the mount before the LORD. And, behold, the LORD passed by, and a great and strong wind rent the mountains, and brake in pieces the rocks before the LORD; but the LORD was not in the wind: and after the wind

an earthquake; but the LORD was not in the earthquake: And after the earthquake a fire; but the LORD was not in the fire: and after the fire a still small voice.

Through nature—

Psalm 19:1 To the chief Musician, A Psalm of David. The heavens declare the glory of God; and the firmament sheweth his handywork.[23]

Romans 1:20 For the invisible things of him from the creation of the world are clearly seen, being understood by the things that are made, even his eternal power and Godhead; so that they are without excuse:

Through wise counsel—

Proverbs 11:14 Where no counsel is, the people fall: but in the multitude of counsellors there is safety.

Proverbs 15:22 Without counsel purposes are disappointed: but in the multitude of counsellors they are established.

Through Scripture—

2 Timothy 3:16-17 All scripture is given by inspiration of God, and is profitable for doctrine, for reproof, for correction, for instruction in righteousness: That the man of God may be perfect, throughly furnished unto all good works.

Through the past—

Psalm 77:10-15 And I said, This is my infirmity: but I will remember the years of the right hand

---

23 Nature provides a sanctuary where I speak and listen to God. There are some walking and skiing trails through the woods where I go to walk or to snowshoe. I am able to be alone, far from the pressures of civilization to pray and to meditate on the Word and the work that the Lord is trying to do in my life. As I walk through the creation I am drawn to the Creator.

of the most High. I will remember the works of the LORD: surely I will remember thy wonders of old. I will meditate also of all thy work, and talk of thy doings. Thy way, O God, is in the sanctuary: who is so great a God as our God? Thou art the God that doest wonders: thou hast declared thy strength among the people. Thou hast with thine arm redeemed thy people, the sons of Jacob and Joseph. Selah.

Through the Holy Spirit's leading—

John 16:13 Howbeit when he, the Spirit of truth, is come, he will guide you into all truth: for he shall not speak of himself; but whatsoever he shall hear, that shall he speak: and he will shew you things to come.

It is essential that we continue in prayer through the times of our darkest grief but it does little good to pray if we do not listen for His answer. He has promised to hear our prayers, we must trust Him to be faithful.

Chapter 5

Don't Be Afraid of the Dark

I remember as a young boy calling my parents into my bedroom in the middle of the night to check for alligators under my bed. My mother would come in, make an obligatory check, and pronounce me safe (at least until she closed the door and the lights went out.) This was before the day of nightlights but my father never would have sprung for the cost of electricity to keep such a frivolous gadget going all night anyway. Looking at it from my perspective, I believed without reservation that a young boy, raised in a middle class family in Northern Michigan should not have to put up with alligators under his bed. My father thought a few alligator bites were better than the cost of a light.

It seems as though most Christians who live in the United States of America believe that we should be exempt from troubles and tribulations. Many of us have been told, "just come to the Cross, accept Jesus Christ as Savior and all of your troubles will be over." We think the Christian life should be free from alligators.

May I share a news flash with you? The Christian life is not free of alligators! Jesus Christ stated it bluntly when He said, *"In the world ye shall have tribulation"*[24] (emphasis added). Throughout the Old and New Testaments we read the stories of men and women who faced terribly difficult trials. We can read 2 Corinthians 11 for Paul's account of his tribulations; 1 Samuel for David's trials with Saul; the Psalms for Asaph's woes, Hebrews 11 for the trials of saints down through the ages and so on throughout the Scriptures.

The question the Lord hears most often must be "why?" But at some point in our grief we must ask the other question, "what?" "What does God want to accomplish in me through this?" What does God want to accomplish through me because of this?"

We begin to understand that the "why" question will never be answered to our satisfaction. The "what" question has difficult, yet more satisfactory answers.

And God may be asking the "who" question while we are stuck on "why?" KC

Even though most of us know those stories we still have the irrepressible feeling that they are for long ago; that they are not for us today. I have been there. Not only with the alligators under my bed but with the alligators of life. I have faced the dark days and dark nights stretching into dark months and dark years. Looking ahead to those years firmly entrenched in my ivory tower I knew that even if I might have to experience difficult times that I was smart enough and spiritual enough to handle them with ease. Looking

---

24 John 16:33 These things I have spoken unto you, that in me ye might have peace. In the world ye shall have tribulation: but be of good cheer; I have overcome the world.

back at those years from my spiritual hospital bed and broken spirit I have no such arrogance. I didn't fear the dark times before because I thought I was too smart and I don't fear the dark times now (very much) because I know God has a purpose in all that He does and He always keeps His promises.

The dark times of life are difficult, and they can be especially difficult in the night when we are alone with our thoughts and our fears.

In the Dark of the Night

Anyone can be joyful when life is going well, but there are those dark times, those difficult times, when we need a song to cheer our heart and our soul. The Psalms were that for the people of Israel. Many of us know that it is in the night, while lying in our bed that the attacks of Satan come. Our mind is weary, our body is tired, and we are alone. The burdens that oppress us during the day seem even heavier at night.

> *Psalm 6:6-7 I am weary with my groaning; all the night make I my bed to swim; I water my couch with my tears. Mine eye is consumed because of grief; it waxeth old because of all mine enemies.*

> *Psalm 77:2-4 In the day of my trouble I sought the Lord: my sore ran in the night, and ceased not: my soul refused to be comforted. I remembered God, and was troubled: I complained, and my spirit was overwhelmed. Selah. Thou holdest mine eyes waking: I am so troubled that I cannot speak.*

> *Job 7:3-4 So am I made to possess months of vanity, and wearisome nights are appointed to me. When I lie down, I say, When shall I arise, and the night be gone? and I am full of tossings to and fro unto the dawning of the day.*

Both widows and widowers have told me that they have slept in a living room chair ever since their spouse died months or even years previous because the empty bed only reminded them of how alone they really were. Night is a lonely time—especially for grievers.

There is Hope

There is hope! The night times and the dark times are not lived apart from the presence of God. We know that since Acts chapter 2 the Holy Spirit indwells the children of God and does so without exception.[25] Instead of Jesus walking with the disciples, He gave the new Church the gift of the indwelling Holy Spirit to comfort God's children.

> All changes, even the most longed for, have their melancholy; for what we leave behind is a part of ourselves; we must die to one life before we can enter another.
>
> Anatole France

What am I to do when the nights are dark and long and I am lonely and afraid?

I can pray—

Psalm 42:8 Yet the LORD will command his lovingkindness in the daytime, and in the night his song shall be with me, and my prayer unto the God of my life.

---

25   John 14:16-17 And I will pray the Father, and he shall give you another Comforter, that he may abide with you for ever; Even the Spirit of truth; whom the world cannot receive, because it seeth him not, neither knoweth him: but ye know him; for he dwelleth with you, and shall be in you.

Ephesians 1:13-14 In whom ye also trusted, after that ye heard the word of truth, the gospel of your salvation: in whom also after that ye believed, ye were sealed with that holy Spirit of promise, Which is the earnest of our inheritance until the redemption of the purchased possession, unto the praise of his glory.

I can meditate—

Psalm 63:5-7 My soul shall be satisfied as with marrow and fatness; and my mouth shall praise thee with joyful lips: When I remember thee upon my bed, and meditate on thee in the night watches. Because thou hast been my help, therefore in the shadow of thy wings will I rejoice.

Psalm 119:148 Mine eyes prevent the night watches, that I might meditate in thy word.

I can recount His works—

Psalm 40:4 Blessed is that man that maketh the LORD his trust, and respecteth not the proud, nor such as turn aside to lies. Many, O LORD my God, are thy wonderful works which thou hast done, and thy thoughts which are to us-ward: they cannot be reckoned up in order unto thee: if I would declare and speak of them, they are more than can be numbered.

I can trust—

Psalm 91:2-6 I will say of the LORD, He is my refuge and my fortress: my God; in him will I trust. Surely he shall deliver thee from the snare of the fowler, and from the noisome pestilence. He shall cover thee with his feathers, and under his wings shalt thou trust: his truth shall be thy shield and buckler. Thou shalt not be afraid for the terror by night; nor for the arrow that flieth by day; Nor for the pestilence that walketh in darkness; nor for the destruction that wasteth at noonday.

I can know that God is good—

Psalm 145:9-10 The LORD is good to all: and his tender mercies are over all his works. All thy works shall praise thee, O LORD; and thy saints shall bless thee.

I can know that God is in control—He causes nations to rise or fall

Job 12:23 He increaseth the nations, and destroyeth them: he enlargeth the nations, and straiteneth them again.

I can give thanks—

Psalm 92:1-5 A Psalm or Song for the sabbath day. It is a good thing to give thanks unto the LORD, and to sing praises unto thy name, O most High: To shew forth thy lovingkindness in the morning, and thy faithfulness every night, Upon an instrument of ten strings, and upon the psaltery; upon the harp with a solemn sound. For thou, LORD, hast made me glad through thy work: I will triumph in the works of thy hands. O LORD, how great are thy works! and thy thoughts are very deep.

God's promises are sure regardless of what we face in life, they are unshakable no matter what mountains of life's evidence seem to point to the contrary and no matter how dark the night gets.

Psalm 139:11-12 If I say, Surely the darkness shall cover me; even the night shall be light about me. Yea, the darkness hideth not from thee; but the night shineth as the day: the darkness and the light are both alike to thee.

The God who spoke light and dark into existence is as faithful to His children in the dark times and the night times as He is in the light. We may not be able to see in the dark—but our Father can.

Chapter 6

Have Faith, Even When It Makes No Sense

Most people who have studied the Psalms point out that many of them begin with some calamity the psalmist is facing, then recount reasons to have faith in God and end with verses praising God for His faithfulness and grace. Psalm 88 is an exception to that unwritten rule. This is a sad psalm from beginning to end. Heman has not seen many good days and if he has seen good days he can't remember any of them at this point in his life. There is no joyful response at the end of Heman's song, it starts out sad and it continues to get more sad as it goes along.

> *A Song or Psalm for the sons of Korah, to the chief Musician upon Mahalath Leannoth, Maschil of Heman the Ezrahite. O LORD God of my salvation, I have cried day and night before thee: (2) Let my prayer come before thee: incline thine ear unto my cry; (3) For my soul is full of troubles: and my life draweth nigh unto the grave. (4) I am counted with them that go down into the pit: I am as a man that hath no strength:*

(5) Free among the dead, like the slain that lie in the grave, whom thou rememberest no more: and they are cut off from thy hand. (6) Thou hast laid me in the lowest pit, in darkness, in the deeps. (7) Thy wrath lieth hard upon me, and thou hast afflicted me with all thy waves. Selah. (8) Thou hast put away mine acquaintance far from me; thou hast made me an abomination unto them: I am shut up, and I cannot come forth. (9) Mine eye mourneth by reason of affliction: LORD, I have called daily upon thee, I have stretched out my hands unto thee. (10) Wilt thou shew wonders to the dead? shall the dead arise and praise thee? Selah. (11) Shall thy lovingkindness be declared in the grave? or thy faithfulness in destruction? (12) Shall thy wonders be known in the dark? and thy righteousness in the land of forgetfulness? (13) But unto thee have I cried, O LORD; and in the morning shall my prayer prevent thee. (14) LORD, why castest thou off my soul? why hidest thou thy face from me? (15) I am afflicted and ready to die from my youth up: while I suffer thy terrors I am distracted. (16) Thy fierce wrath goeth over me; thy terrors have cut me off. (17) They came round about me daily like water; they compassed me about together. (18) Lover and friend hast thou put far from me, and mine acquaintance into darkness. Psalm 88

Can you imagine a song leader in a church today suggesting that we sing this Psalm some Sunday morning? The organist would begin a mournful introduction and the congregation in monotone would slowly sing through Heman's soul-wrenching words, certainly not the type of music most of us like to sing.

I am a fan of movies about the old west. I enjoy cowboy movies where the hero fights his way through a tough situation that only he can handle, defeats the bad guys showing a clear difference between good and evil and then rides off into the sunset (with or without the girl) as the credits roll slowly across the screen. There are movies, however, where the hero does not define right and wrong quite so clearly or he dies before the end of the movie. I do not enjoy those and hardly ever watch them more than once.

We expect a happy ending in Psalm 88 where the hero, Heman the Ezrahite, closes the psalm with praise to God for deliverance. That happy ending never comes. Heman closes his writing as he began with the fact that life is hard. Shouldn't the Bible only present the positive elements of following God? Isn't that what we do when we are trying to win someone to the Lord? We only tell them about the cross that Jesus had to carry but never about the cross we, His children are to carry.

On this side of the cross, we have a greater perspective than Heman did. Even in the depths of our despair we know the Living Hope, Jesus Christ our Lord and Savior.[26] We know that this life is not all there is. A skeptic would say there is no evidence of a happy ending in the words of this Psalm but we, seeing the big picture from this side of the cross, know there is one. A perspective that sees no farther than the grave is an incomplete glance at the life of the believer.

Why Would the Holy Spirit Inspire This Morose Song?

God is the God of truth, a theme that pervades the Scriptures from cover to cover. He desires truth

---

26   1 Peter 1:3 Blessed be the God and Father of our Lord Jesus Christ, which according to his abundant mercy hath begotten us again unto a lively hope by the resurrection of Jesus Christ from the dead,

from His children as we express the thoughts of our heart to Him. He could handle Heman's honest words and He can handle our honesty as well. We always should go to God in truth and in reverent fear (Exodus 18:21, Joshua 24:14, 1 Samuel 12:24,

> Peace is not the absence of trials but is the presence of God.
> Unknown

Psalms 86:11, Proverbs 16:6). We learn from Psalm 88 that God wants us to come and pray to Him all of the time, not just on the days when we sing happy songs but also on those days when we sing sad, even morose songs. Heman's example to us is that we can go to God with anything—anytime.

We expect the trials we go through to all make sense to us in the here and now. Sometimes we must wait for eternity to see the other side of the tapestry; [27] to see in hindsight what God has seen in foresight. There is an old saying that my mother repeated to me many times, "God is still on the throne—and He ain't nervous." It may help us to envision God sitting upon heaven's throne with no hint of sweat on His brow nor fear in His heart. He is in control—and He is good.

God's ways are not our ways. Why should they be? Why would we expect them to be? He is all-knowing and all-wise and we have limited knowledge and limited wisdom. None of us would want a god who is as weak as we are.

Isaiah 55:8-9 For my thoughts are not your thoughts, neither are your ways my ways, saith

---

27 There is a well-known story about a young child who sees only the back side of the tapestry and wonders why someone would make such an ugly thing. When the mother turns the tapestry over the beauty is revealed. So it is to be in our life when we finally see the other side, the one only the Lord sees at this time.

the LORD. For as the heavens are higher than the earth, so are my ways higher than your ways, and my thoughts than your thoughts.

1 Corinthians 1:25 Because the foolishness of God is wiser than men; and the weakness of God is stronger than men.

How many of us who have read the story of Joseph for the first time with his being sold into slavery by his brothers and all the trouble that he went through with Potiphar's wife, prison, his dreams, etc. would anticipate his words to his brothers in Genesis 50:20 *"But as for you, ye thought evil against me; but God meant it unto good, to bring to pass, as it is this day, to save much people alive."*

We see no such reward coming to Heman at the end of his Psalm, however, he calls upon God day and night and never mentions quitting. If we have to go through a trial every so often we want it to be short, learn a quick lesson and get on with life. Sometimes there are trials that do not end right away. Some trials will have no end in this lifetime such as when we face the death of an only child; the prognosis of Alzheimer's or the diagnosis of a terminal illness. It is at that time that we write songs like Heman did in Psalm 88 or we read his words and claim them as our own.

Heman teaches us to choose faith even when life seems hopeless; that faith in God is better than despair; that our calls to God night and day are not falling on deaf ears. He teaches us to not walk away from the faith and from God. He is an example of praying without ceasing.

Heman's past was difficult, his present is horrible but he still has hope even if it is not expressed. Even though he has lived a lifetime in the depths of the valley he cries out to God. If I have lost hope and given up on God there is no reason to pray—why pray if God doesn't seem to hear our prayers? Why pray if He hears but does not answer?

We do not live in a world where all will be made right here and they 'lived happily ever after'. The wife whose husband is in the middle stages of Alzheimer's, the parents whose newborn has Down's syndrome and the person who has lived for thirty years with quadriplegia all know that, short of a miracle, there is no hope in this life of recovery. But even in the midst of all of that the child of God can choose hope.

Nowhere in the Scriptures do the writers say, "I am going through difficult problems but when I look at other people and see how bad their problems are, I guess I am doing okay." God does not allow trials into our life to get us to compare our lives with other people; He allows us to face trials to cause us to look to Him. KC

The Living Hope promises:

◊ There is perfect peace available to us now that only God can give

◊ There is comfort that flows to us

◊ There can be meaningful ministry that flows from God through us

◊ That our Heavenly Father cares for us.

◊ That in the life to come that all of this world's wrongs will be made right

◊ That there is a new body in the next life that will cause us to forget all about this weak vessel that we now claim as home.

Looking around there is little if any hope but looking up there is hope in abundance.

Why Does God Not Answer?

Verse 14 of Psalm 88 is a troubling verse *"LORD, why castest thou off my soul? why hidest thou thy face from me?"* It reminds us of Job in his time of distress:

> *Job 23:8-9 Behold, I go forward, but he is not there; and backward, but I cannot perceive him: On the left hand, where he doth work, but I cannot behold him: he hideth himself on the right hand, that I cannot see him:*

> *Job 30:20 I cry unto thee, and thou dost not hear me: I stand up, and thou regardest me not.*

Both Heman and Job have experienced times when it seems as though God just does not hear their prayers. It reminds us of a posting on Facebook that says, "The teacher is always silent during the test."

God is always speaking but maybe He is doing like Christ did so often and is answering the question we did not ask but should have. Jesus sometimes answered a question with a question.[28] Maybe God is responding to our questions with one of His own, "Will you trust Me even where there is overwhelming evidence not to?" Sometimes He speaks the same words to us that He did to the father whose daughter had died, *"Be not afraid, only believe."*

> *Mark 5:35-36 While he yet spake, there came from the ruler of the synagogue's house certain which said, Thy daughter is dead: why troublest*

28 Matthew 9:14-15 Then came to him the disciples of John, saying, Why do we and the Pharisees fast oft, but thy disciples fast not? And Jesus said unto them, Can the children of the bridechamber mourn, as long as the bridegroom is with them? but the days will come, when the bridegroom shall be taken from them, and then shall they fast.

thou the Master any further? As soon as Jesus heard the word that was spoken, he saith unto the ruler of the synagogue, Be not afraid, only believe.

There are also times when He doesn't seem to answer at all. Does He speak from the past in those times? Is that why there is a Psalm 77, 78 or 136 where the psalmist recounts God's mighty works in the days of Moses and others? In the times when God is silent we are to go back to Scripture and be reminded of the attributes of God; we are to pull out our journals and recount how God used to speak to us, being confident that He will do so again.

What to Choose?

Heman seemingly has no reason to believe in God. Nothing is working well in his life. He is near death surrounded by corpses. All of his acquaintances are like they are dead to him (Verse 5), his family and friends are no comfort in his time of long trial (Verse 8). Yet he cries out to the God of his salvation, he cries out night and day (Verse 1). He is 'praying without ceasing' because, as bad as his life is, he knows the only answer comes from God.

> It never cost a disciple anything to follow Jesus: to talk about cost when you are in love with someone is an insult.
>
> Oswald Chambers

Psalm 121:1-2 A Song of degrees. I will lift up mine eyes unto the hills, from whence cometh my help. My help cometh from the LORD, which made heaven and earth.

Few people would have blamed Heman if he had walked away. We all know what it is like to have people disappoint us. We may have had family or close friends or fellow church members who have ignored us in the time of our deepest agony. When God seemed silent, Heman says he is like those that lie in the grave *"whom thou rememberest no more"*, and yet in spite of all of that he continues to call out to God. Many of us have faith when the days are sunny but Heman has it when all of his days are as black as coal.

Some of us have been through periods of depression in our spiritual lives and can identify with the Psalmist. He doesn't mention anything good going on in his life. His life is full of trials and he is near death, he has lost all strength to cope with life and feels as one of the dead. It seems as though God has cut him off from Himself and his friends. He is an 'abomination' to his friends. Maybe he felt like Job comparing the time when life was good, to his condition now:

> *Job 29:7-10 When I went out to the gate through the city, when I prepared my seat in the street! The young men saw me, and hid themselves: and the aged arose, and stood up. The princes refrained talking, and laid their hand on their mouth. The nobles held their peace, and their tongue cleaved to the roof of their mouth....(Job 30:1) But now they that are younger than I have me in derision, whose fathers I would have disdained to have set with the dogs of my flock.*

Does God Promise an Easy Life for His Children?

Is the believer promised an easy life? Job, Heman (Psalm 88), Paul (Acts 9:16, 1 Corinthians 11) and the saints of Hebrews 11 say no.

Heman, the writer of Psalm 88, is never mentioned in Scripture as having anything to say except for this Psalm. His cries, however, were not falling on deaf or uncaring ears; his cries were actually God-breathed into Scripture and are heard again by Him every time one of His children reads them with a broken heart.

Did God help him speak those words, which almost seem blasphemous for my benefit? While the Nation of Israel never came to Heman's side to support him, his words were written down to be sung as comfort to them; his words were to be sung by them in the darkest times of their exile. Heman's words are also written for saints today, for you and me, to sing in our darkest times.

Chapter 7

God is in Control And He is Good.

God has a purpose in our trials. He allows us to go through them for a reason. We must look for the Lord in the depths of our despair, grow in Him, and learn every truth we possibly can. God's wisdom and His ways do not always make sense to the idle observer. They certainly don't make sense to the one whose life is falling apart around them.

God is Enough—Or is He?

Any time we begin to identify ourselves as, "Hi, I'm Jim, I am a widower" or "My name is Sally, I am the mother of a daughter who died," we are saying that God is not enough. That He is not enough to fill the void in our life left by that person whom we loved so dearly. We essentially say that, "God is good, and we love Him, but He is not enough to mend our broken heart."

This is not to say that a parent whose child has died is going to grieve for a set period of time and then move on like that child never lived. A father said recently that he was afraid to stop grieving his son because if he did, his son's name would never be mentioned again. He said he loved hearing his son's name and he appreciated it when friends would tell stories about his son—and then added, 'but they don't do that anymore and I am afraid that if I stop grieving my son will be forgotten.'

It is not that we don't grieve; it is not that there is not a hole in our heart, it is not that there is not an empty place, real or figuratively, at the Christmas dinner table but our grief should never look just like the grief of the unsaved. We should be able to say, "my child died, but..." And the 'but' should lead up to the fact that the Living Hope, Christ Jesus, is enough to cause us to look forward to a time when all will be made right and death and sin will never claim another victory over anyone.

"My grace is sufficient."[29] That is a promise that covers any area of our life that requires grace. For me to say that God's grace is big enough for your grief but not for mine only states without equivocation that my estimation of God is too small and my estimation of my trial is too large. I am placing myself above God's ability to bring hope, joy and peace into my life.

We remember when Sarah tried to help God keep the promise He had made to Abraham about giving him a son. To those of us reading that story thousands of years later and knowing its outcome, we are mildly amused at Abraham's and then Sarah's struggles with the promise that she would give birth to a son even though they were well past child-bearing

29 2 Corinthians 12:9 And he said unto me, My grace is sufficient for thee: for my strength is made perfect in weakness. Most gladly therefore will I rather glory in my infirmities, that the power of Christ may rest upon me.

years. Finally Sarah invents a plan to help God out of the mess (in her mind) He had gotten Himself into by making a promise He didn't seem able to keep. Her plan was that Abraham would have the son by Sarah's handmaid Hagar. Abraham and Hagar did have a son but it was not the son God had promised and, in God's perfect timing, Sarah did conceive and bear a son. The world still bears the weight of that sin, of someone trying to help God keep His promise.

> *2 Corinthians 1:3-5 Blessed be God, even the Father of our Lord Jesus Christ, the Father of mercies, and the God of all comfort; Who comforteth us in all our tribulation, that we may be able to comfort them which are in any trouble, by the comfort wherewith we ourselves are comforted of God. For as the sufferings of Christ abound in us, so our consolation also aboundeth by Christ.*

God promises to comfort us in all our tribulation. And He comforts us so *"that we may be able to comfort them which are in any trouble."* These promises are made by the same God who made the promise to Abraham that he would have a son. Why do we believe the promises less when they are made to us than when we read Abraham's story? Abraham and Sarah gave birth to the son of promise even though they were well beyond child-bearing years. God will keep His promise to us for comfort even when our heart is broken, seemingly beyond repair.

God Keeps His Promises

Can you imagine what the Christian life would be like if God kept only a portion of His promises? If He wrote in the preface of the Bible that He will keep 90% of the promises that He made but He didn't tell us which ones He will not keep? How would we know which ones to believe? Which ones to cling to when our lives are being battered by the storms of life? Which ones about His imminent return for His children are true?

In those times of our deepest grief the writer of Hebrews reminds us that God cannot lie and because of that, He is the faithful refuge in our darkest times. He is the sure and steadfast anchor for our soul. God is the Friend who always keeps all of His promises— even to Abraham and Sarah and even to you and me in our darkest trials.

> *Hebrews 6:17-19 Wherein God, willing more abundantly to shew unto the heirs of promise the immutability of his counsel, confirmed it by an oath: That by two immutable things, in which it was impossible for God to lie, we might have a strong consolation, who have fled for refuge to lay hold upon the hope set before us: Which hope we have as an anchor of the soul, both sure and stedfast, and which entereth into that within the veil;*

God's Promises

All of God's promises,[30] even the ones that have already been fulfilled, are for those of us living today. They reveal God's character and the fact that He keeps His promises. His promises to love and to care for His people may have been given to David as he wrote the Psalms but they are for you and me today when we are in need of that same love and care.

---

30 Dr. Jon M. Jenkins said in a sermon, "Not all of God's promises are TO me but all of God's promises are FOR me." All of the promises that God has made and kept are FOR me in that they reveal the character of God. But the promise to Abraham for a son or to Sampson for strength are not TO me. I will not have a son of promise as did Abraham and Sarah and as much as I would like to have the physical prowess of Sampson I am afraid that will never happen.

The question is: do we believe God will keep His promises? I don't mean do we give mental ascent to the fact that God has kept a lot of promises in the past to the Nation of Israel but do we stake our life and our health on the fact that God will always keep His promises for us today?

Do we believe, in spite of what seems to be evidence to the contrary, that God is in control and that He is good? Many of us believe that God is good but still wonder—if He is good, how could He be in control of this world in chaos? There seems to be too much evil around us, it comes in waves; the waves get deeper and they seem to overwhelm us and call God's control and His goodness into question.

> A Song of degrees. They that trust in the LORD shall be as mount Zion, which cannot be removed, but abideth for ever. As the mountains are round about Jerusalem, so the LORD is round about his people from henceforth even for ever. Psalm 125:1-2

God Keeps His promises in His Time

God's promises never get too difficult for Him to keep. He didn't breathe a sigh of relief when Sarah suggested that maybe Hagar could bear the promised son. We should understand however that there are promises without condition but there are others that have one or more conditions attached. One of my all-time favorite, most comforting verses is found in the book of Deuteronomy.

> *Deuteronomy 33:27a The eternal God is thy refuge, and underneath are the everlasting arms:*

That promise is true whether I can feel His arms underneath me or not. In my dark times I prayed that God would help me to feel the arms. I knew they were there because He said they were, but I couldn't feel them. I was at a point in my life when I couldn't 'feel' much of anything except for anger, self-pity and other products of my hard heart. But I knew that God promised that His arms were underneath me. For the child of God there are no conditions attached to that promise.

Another one of my most comforting verses is Isaiah 26:3. I felt the overwhelming comfort of this promise when I claimed it during the final two days of my father's life on earth.

Isaiah 26:3 Thou wilt keep him in perfect peace, whose mind is stayed on thee: because he trusteth in thee.

Our Heavenly Father promises perfect peace for His children—but only if we trust Him. God does not say He will keep us in perfect peace if our problem is not too large or if other people cooperate. He promises peace if we trust. Trusting in God yields perfect peace. Lack of trust in God yields no peace.

God Is Faithful

The Scriptures are replete with the reminder that God is faithful and that He will keep every promise that He makes. We can believe His promise of a plan for us, of watch care, of peace and the availability of joy during life's greatest hardships because He is faithful.

1 Thessalonians 5:23-24 And the very God of peace sanctify you wholly; and I pray God your whole spirit and soul and body be preserved blameless unto the coming of our Lord Jesus

Christ. Faithful is he that calleth you, who also will do it.

2 Timothy 2:13 If we believe not, yet he abideth faithful: he cannot deny himself.

God wants to heal our broken heart. Second Corinthians teaches us that He is the God of all comfort.[31] The Psalms teach us of His protection, that His hand is upon us and that He is the perfect refuge for the Believer.[32] Deuteronomy teaches us of His sheltering arms.[33] The Book of Isaiah teaches us that He will provide daily strength to enable us to soar with the wings of eagles.[34] The entire Word of God teaches us of His love for us.

Our trials may bring scars but God has a purpose in them. When others see the scars and that our faith is not shaken, they are pointed not to us but to the Comforter.

2 Corinthians 4:7 But we have this treasure in earthen vessels, that the excellency of the power may be of God, and not of us.

---

31   2 Corinthians 1:3-4 Blessed be God, even the Father of our Lord Jesus Christ, the Father of mercies, and the God of all comfort; Who comforteth us in all our tribulation, that we may be able to comfort them which are in any trouble, by the comfort wherewith we ourselves are comforted of God.

32   Psalm 59:16 But I will sing of thy power; yea, I will sing aloud of thy mercy in the morning: for thou hast been my defence and refuge in the day of my trouble.

33   Deuteronomy 33:27 The eternal God is thy refuge, and underneath are the everlasting arms: and he shall thrust out the enemy from before thee; and shall say, Destroy them.

34   Isaiah 40:29-31 He giveth power to the faint; and to them that have no might he increaseth strength. Even the youths shall faint and be weary, and the young men shall utterly fall: But they that wait upon the LORD shall renew their strength; they shall mount up with wings as eagles; they shall run, and not be weary; and they shall walk, and not faint

God Promises To Work Good

A pastor once told me of his mother's time in an assisted-living facility and concluded by saying, "I defy anyone to show me any good that can come from this." It is easy for those who are only casual observers to say to this man, "count it all joy when you face trials" or "God promises to work good out of all things" and go back to their flowery beds of ease.[35] The husband standing beside the bed of a wife who has not spoken in five years might find it a little more difficult to see God's goodness than does the young bride and groom showered with birdseed on their way out of the church. What happened to the person he walked down the aisle with, to go out and conquer life with and to grow old with? The joy of that wedding night seems far distant as his beloved 'better half' walks off to an unknown land where he cannot follow.

God does not make promises that He cannot or will not keep. The promises that God made to Adam and Eve in the Garden are still being kept by Him. The promises He made to Abraham are still being fulfilled. The promise, made throughout the Scriptures *"he will not fail thee, nor forsake thee"*[36] is just as true for the person in the throes of a dreaded disease as they were when first uttered to God's people as they prepared to cross the Jordan River.

God promises to work good but we don't always

---

35 "Must I be carried to the skies, On flowery beds of ease, While others fought to win the prize, And sailed through bloody seas?" Second verse of "Am I A Soldier of the Cross?" written by Isaac Watts

36 Deuteronomy 31:6 Be strong and of a good courage, fear not, nor be afraid of them: for the LORD thy God, he it is that doth go with thee; he will not fail thee, nor forsake thee.

agree with Him as to what 'good' looks like.[37] Cassie Bernal, one of the students killed at Columbine High School, prayed to be a missionary and to spread the Gospel. She died at the hand of a fellow student before she ever wore her graduation cap and gown. Her prayers were answered however when millions of people heard the Gospel story as men of God preached the Word at her funeral which was broadcast nationwide. But Cassie died and her family grieves.

A prodigal daughter goes off to experience life without limits while the family and the church pray for her return. Eventually she returns home, pregnant and unrepentant. The family is thankful she is home, they love the new baby but would anyone ever choose this? Is this good?

We are left to the Lord's mercy as to what 'good' will look like. Very seldom is it what we would have prayed for. Neither Cassie Bernal nor the family of the prodigal would have expected their prayers to be answered in the way they were. They may have prayed differently had they known what God's 'good' looked like.

My mother's greatest fear was spending the last days of her life in an assisted-care facility. She tried by every means available to her to avoid that. To have her go into a care facility was also one of her children's greatest fears, we were afraid for how angry she would be and how that anger might overflow. One Sunday morning we went to her house to pick her up for church but she didn't come to the door and she didn't respond to the doorbell. When I entered the house I found her in her bedroom; she had experienced a

---

37   See the story in the Appendix entitled "The Prayer Meeting." It is a fictional story based on true Bible stories of individuals who never would have prayed for the tragedy they experienced yet the result of that tragedy was God's glory and their growth.

stroke earlier that morning and could only stay in bed and await our arrival. She lived one month after her stroke but it was a blessed month. Her mind had been affected so she did not dread the care facility and the Lord used that month for healing within the family. I journaled my way through that time and every so often go back and reread that journal. I marvel at the lessons the Lord was teaching and at the work He was doing in many lives and on many levels.

Would anyone in our family have prayed for my mother to have a stroke? Absolutely not. Would anyone have thought that a stroke would have been a way to accomplish good? Absolutely not. In fact we would have thought a stroke would have made matters worse. But that is exactly what the Lord used to accomplish much good for His purposes and in many lives.

Does God Send Trials or Allow Them?

Do trials come from God? Does He allow them or do they only come from our sin? Heman certainly attributes his trials to God as do others. Chapters one and two of the book of Job teach that Satan plays an active role in our trials, but only to the extent that God allows. Satan addresses that in Job chapter one:

> *Job 1:10-11 Hast not thou made an hedge about him, and about his house, and about all that he hath on every side? thou hast blessed the work of his hands, and his substance is increased in the land. But put forth thine hand now, and touch all that he hath, and he will curse thee to thy face.*

Satan acknowledges the fact that God has placed a hedge about Job, his house and all that he owns, but then he dares God to take his hand of blessing away and suffer Job's anger. Reading through those first two chapters of Job we see that the hedge varies in size, at first encompassing *"all that he hath"* and later protecting only Job's life.

There is a tension that exists between attributing the death of Job's children to God or to Satan. A Petoskey poet wrote the following poem in 1883 at the death of a 16 year-old young man. This was the third death of a child under the age of 21 to this same family.

Through misty shadows hope is born,
Which soothes the weary sigh,
And woos to slumber while the morn
Breaks o'er the eastern sky.

It bids us dry the dimming tear
And cease the bitter moan,
Then sweetly lisps these words of cheer,
He taketh but His own.

His tender lambs He gathers in,
And though our hearts are sore,
We know that from a world of sin
He shields them evermore.

And yet the parting's bitter still,
The way seems dark and drear;
We cannot see the milestones till
The clouds shall disappear.

But in that blissful future when
We'll reunited be,
With those we've loved, the meeting then
From sorrow shall be free.

Then we shall fully understand
The mystery none can tell,
How God afflicts by His own hand,
Yet doeth all things well.[38]

The last two lines of the poem always cause me to stop and think of the majesty of God. How can God allow a loved one to die or allow us to suffer some heart-wrenching loss *"yet doeth all things well"*?

The atheist asks two questions that every Christian answers in the affirmative: Is God good? Yes. Is He all-powerful? Yes. The atheist's position is that if God is good then He would stamp evil from the earth unless He cannot do so. If He cannot stamp evil out of existence then He is not all-powerful. Their premise is that God cannot be both good and all-powerful at the same time.

The Christian believes that God can allow trials in our life and be so good and so powerful that He can make even the calamity of our most egregious trial good. (Romans 8:28, Genesis 50:20.)

This is proven by Job in the last chapter of his story. After he had suffered unimaginable loss and grief he repented for ever questioning God and he acknowledged that the trials he faced had caused him to grow in the Lord.

> *Job 42:5-6 I have heard of thee by the hearing of the ear: but now mine eye seeth thee. Wherefore I abhor myself, and repent in dust and ashes.*

It is also proven by the Apostle Paul after he had asked the Lord to remove the thorn in the flesh that made his life and ministry so difficult. God cannot only make trials to work together for good but He can make them into something that we praise Him for.

38   Lelia M. Rowan, October 3, 1883

Psalm 119:71 It is good for me that I have been afflicted; that I might learn thy statutes.

And it is proven by Christians around the world as God's work in their broken lives teach His goodness and faithfulness in a powerful, living sermon.

Hear me speedily, O LORD: my spirit faileth: hide not thy face from me, lest I be like unto them that go down into the pit. Cause me to hear thy lovingkindness in the morning; for in thee do I trust: cause me to know the way wherein I should walk; for I lift up my soul unto thee. Deliver me, O LORD, from mine enemies: I flee unto thee to hide me. Teach me to do thy will; for thou art my God: thy spirit is good; lead me into the land of uprightness. Quicken me, O LORD, for thy name's sake: for thy righteousness' sake bring my soul out of trouble. Psalm 143:7-11

To the chief Musician upon Jonathelemrechokim, Michtam of David, when the Philistines took him in Gath. Be merciful unto me, O God: for man would swallow me up; he fighting daily oppresseth me. Mine enemies would daily swallow me up: for they be many that fight against me, O thou most High. What time I am afraid, I will trust in thee. In God I will praise his word, in God I have put my trust; I will not fear what flesh can do unto me. Every day they wrest my words: all their thoughts are against me for evil. They gather themselves together, they hide themselves, they mark my steps, when they wait for my soul. Shall they escape by iniquity? in thine anger cast down the people, O God. Thou tellest my wanderings: put thou my tears into thy bottle: are they not in thy book? When I cry unto thee, then shall mine enemies turn back: this I know; for God is for me. In God will I praise his word: in the LORD will I praise his word. In God have I put my trust: I will not be afraid what man can do unto me. Thy vows are upon me, O God: I will render praises unto thee. For thou hast delivered my soul from death: wilt not thou deliver my feet from falling, that I may walk before God in the light of the living? Psalm 56

Chapter 8

Be Still

Psalm 46 God is our refuge and strength, a very present help in trouble. Therefore will not we fear, though the earth be removed, and though the mountains be carried into the midst of the sea; Though the waters thereof roar and be troubled, though the mountains shake with the swelling thereof. Selah. There is a river, the streams whereof shall make glad the city of God, the holy place of the tabernacles of the most High. God is in the midst of her; she shall not be moved: God shall help her, and that right early. The heathen raged, the kingdoms were moved: he uttered his voice, the earth melted. The Lord of hosts is with us; the God of Jacob is our refuge. Selah. Come, behold the works of the Lord, what desolations he hath made in the earth. He maketh wars to cease unto the end of the earth; he breaketh the bow, and cutteth the spear in sunder; he burneth the chariot in the fire. Be still, and know that I am God: I will be exalted among the heathen, I will be exalted in the earth. The Lord of hosts is with us; the God of Jacob is our refuge. Selah.

The sight of that seething turmoil in Psalm 46, spread out in front of us, threatens to overwhelm us. We are reminded of Gideon's words in another setting, *"if the LORD be with us, why then is all this befallen us?"* [39] How does anyone survive this? All of our hopes and dreams are consumed by the tumult that overwhelms the landscape before us. There is no place to run— we have tried. There is no place to hide, this is our life now, this is our 'new normal.' And into a seemingly overwhelmed life God speaks, *"Be still."*

'Tis far, far better to let
  Him choose
The way that we
  should take;
If only we leave our
  lives to Him
He will guide without
  mistake
We, in our blindness,
  would never choose
A pathway dark and
  rough,
And so we should ever
  find in Him,
"The God Who Is
  Enough."

Tan, P. L. (1996). Encyclopedia of 7700 Illustrations: Signs of the Times (p. 1526). Garland, TX: Bible Communications, Inc.

This is not a 'be still' because there is no hope. This is not a 'be still' because this will all be over in a few minutes. Our Father makes no promises about the intensity or the duration of the storm. His *"still small voice"*[40] heard above the roar of the wind and

---

39 Judges 6:13 And Gideon said unto him, Oh my Lord, if the LORD be with us, why then is all this befallen us? and where be all his miracles which our fathers told us of, saying, Did not the LORD bring us up from Egypt? but now the LORD hath forsaken us, and delivered us into the hands of the Midianites.

40 1 Kings 19:11-12 And he said, Go forth, and stand upon the mount before the LORD. And, behold, the LORD passed by, and a great and strong wind rent the mountains, and brake in pieces the rocks before the LORD; but the LORD was not in the wind: and after the wind an earthquake; but the LORD was not in the earthquake: (12) And after the earthquake a fire; but the LORD was not in the fire: and after the fire a still small voice.

destruction, speaks to the deepest part of our soul—
"Be still."

Those words by themselves would seem out of place, irrelevant, insufficient, if not followed by, *"And know that I am God."* The Creator, the Voice, who spoke all of nature into existence[41] and upholds it all *"by the Word of His power"*[42] is still in control. Imagine being there on the day God created the heavens and the earth. As the Voice spoke, perfectly formed universes were flung out far beyond the reach of man's strongest telescope. Land took shape as snow-capped mountains rose from the surface of earth's globe and water rushed to fill the low places. Majestic trees and delicate flowers sprouted from soil that had not existed only minutes before.

And it is the same Voice that speaks these words, *"Be still, and know that I am God."* He tells us we are safe because we are His. *"When thou passest through the waters, I will be with thee; and through the rivers, they shall not overflow thee: when thou walkest through the fire, thou shalt not be burned; neither shall the flame kindle upon thee."* (Isaiah 43:2)

When none of life makes any sense and our best-laid plans have been ground to powder, God continues to remind us of His unfailing steadfastness with His precious words, *"For I know the thoughts that I think toward you, saith the Lord, thoughts of peace, and not of evil, to give you an expected end."* (Jeremiah 29:11).

It is God Himself that says to *"be still."* It is not the psalmist speaking on God's behalf; it is God Himself

---

41   Genesis 1:3 And God said, Let there be light: and there was light.

42   Hebrews 1:3 Who being the brightness of his glory, and the express image of his person, and upholding all things by the word of his power, when he had by himself purged our sins, sat down on the right hand of the Majesty on high;

who reassures us that no matter what cataclysmic events we may face that He is still God, He is still in control, and He is still good.

Be Still

To 'be still', does not mean to give up, but to trust. It is giving up my need to help God in the fight. It is to cease striving and to let God do the work only He can do.

> *Lamentations 3:22-26 It is of the LORD'S mercies that we are not consumed, because his compassions fail not. They are new every morning: great is thy faithfulness. The LORD is my portion, saith my soul; therefore will I hope in him. The LORD is good unto them that wait for him, to the soul that seeketh him. It is good that a man should both hope and quietly wait for the salvation of the LORD.*

It is in deer hunting that I practice the art of being still. I work at being quiet so as not to arouse the keen senses of the whitetail deer with which I am sharing the woods. I am not merely taking a break from activity; but I watch where I step, I muffle a cough or sneeze, I move slowly. I want to be almost nonexistent in the forest as far as the animals are concerned. I am actively quiet.

I also am actively listening. I am employing my senses to be able to detect the intrusion of a whitetail deer into my space. I want to distinguish all of the noises; is it the fall of a beech nut or the deer's hoof on a frozen leaf? Is it a red squirrel scurrying to find its winter food or is it a deer coming my way? I cannot 'do' anything without disturbing the natural sounds of the forest except to actively watch and listen.

When I hunt I carry a Bible and a notebook; I journal my thoughts as I sit quietly in the woods. I am also actively quiet before God. The Holy Spirit guides my thinking as I take time to ponder the scriptures I have just read. There have been many times I have left the woods thankful that I didn't see a deer which would have distracted me from the best reason to be actively quiet—to hear from God. My efforts at being still allow me better opportunity to hear His 'still small voice.'

This Psalm teaches that God is a very present help in trouble. Because we know He is our Help we can say, *"therefore, we will not fear."* We can say, 'Therefore, God is with us, He is our refuge.' We can say, 'Therefore, the Lord of Hosts is our refuge' because He has promised that for His children.

The name "Lord of Hosts" is an interesting name. He is the Creator and Lord of hosts (legions) of angels. Do you remember when one angel came and killed 185,000 Assyrian soldiers in one night? [43] If the promise was that God and that one angel were watching over us, wouldn't that be enough? And yet God promises us that He and legions of His angels are in charge over us.

Sometimes the Father tells us to be still in the midst of the storm and sometimes He calms the storm. Luke tells the account of the disciples and Jesus in a boat on their way across the Sea of Galilee. A terrible storm arose and the disciples, some of them fisherman who were accustomed to being on rough seas, were afraid for their lives. At the same time that they were afraid Jesus was asleep, seemingly oblivious to the

---

43 2 Kings 19:35 And it came to pass that night, that the angel of the Lord went out, and smote in the camp of the Assyrians an hundred fourscore and five thousand: and when they arose early in the morning, behold, they were all dead corpses.

storm. They woke Jesus, *"And he arose, and rebuked the wind, and said unto the sea, Peace, be still. And the wind ceased, and there was a great calm.*"[44]

These disciples had followed Jesus, they had witnessed miracles, they were in the boat with Him but they didn't know He could speak peace in life-threatening storms. He was their Rabbi but He was not Lord to them.

> *Mark 4:41 What manner of man is this that speaks and waves be still?*

In our grief we must remember that God can calm the storms or He can calm us. He can only calm us if we believe that He is in control—and that He is good.

God Is For Us

How do we know that He is our Help? The Psalmist asks us to behold the works of the Lord. How do we know that God is for us?

> *Romans 8:31-32 What shall we then say to these things? If God be for us, who can be against us? He that spared not his own Son, but delivered him up for us all, how shall he not with him also freely give us all things?*

The same God who has spoken universes into existence—is for us. The same God who protected the Nation of Israel and continues to guard their history—is for us. The same God who protected Paul and Silas, who broke down prison doors for Peter—is for us. The same God who healed the sick and raised the dead—is for us. The same God who could feed 5,000 people with a little boy's lunch—is for us. We can behold His works and believe His promises—He is

---

44   Luke 4:39

94

for us. And if He is for us, who can be against us? [45]

How long do we wait for help to come? He doesn't give a time limit. He does not say to be still for five minutes, or five days, or five months or five decades. He says to *"be still."* *"And know that I am God."* We can be still and wait for as long as it takes because He is God.

In the period my wife and I refer to as our 'black years' there was a portion of one Scripture that I could hold to as my anchor in the faith. When I began to sink into despair I went back to the Psalms and to the first three chapters of Ephesians to find some hope for my life. It was no use, the words that used to thrill my soul were now as reading dust. I was in despair. I didn't know what to do or even what to think. If reading about my position with Christ in the heavenlies didn't do anything for me, what would? Into that time the Lord gave me a portion of one verse: *"The eternal God is thy refuge, and underneath are the everlasting arms:"* (Deuteronomy 33:27a). I clung to that promise unwaveringly and my faith in that portion of one verse and in that one promise made it possible to believe the rest of the Scripture and the rest of God's promises. I knew that if I could believe that promise that I could believe all of them and if that one verse was true then the rest of Scripture was true as well.

I Can Do This on My Own

We all want to feel capable, especially in the basic tasks of life. Jesus understood our propensity to 'go it on our own' when He told His disciples (and

---

45   Romans 8:31 What shall we then say to these things? If God be for us, who can be against us?

us) that *"without me, ye can do nothing"*.[46] Jesus was preparing His disciples for the fact that He was going to be leaving them in a few hours and he gave them instructions on how to live life here on earth.

This passage is usually related to ministry efforts regarding witnessing, preaching or teaching and that is certainly a correct usage. But we need to understand that all of our life is spiritual.[47] If we look carefully at John 15:5 to see what it says about the scope of what we can do without Him, it is all-inclusive: we can do nothing without Him which includes grieving in a way that honors Him.

Why would God want to be involved in helping us grieve properly? Because how we grieve says something about our fellowship with God. We have already discussed Paul's words that we *"don't grieve as those who have no hope."*[48] How we grieve should be instructional to those who are watching on what it means to have hope in Jesus Christ.

The world watches the church for how it responds to practical life situations. In 2006 the world watched in horror at reports of a shooting at yet another school. This time it was an Amish school in Lancaster County, Pennsylvania where ten schoolgirls were shot and five died before the gunman committed suicide. But even more than the horror of the heinous murders, the world took notice of the reaction of the Amish community who forgave the man who had gunned down their daughters. They ministered to the murderer's wife. Money flowed in to the Amish

---

46   John 15:5   I am the vine, ye are the branches: He that abideth in me, and I in him, the same bringeth forth much fruit: for without me ye can do nothing.

47   1 Corinthians 10:31   Whether therefore ye eat, or drink, or whatsoever ye do, do all to the glory of God.

48   1 Thessalonians 4:13

families from around the world as many tried to wrap their minds around the evil that had been committed that day. The Amish shared that money with the wife of the man who had killed their daughters. Hardened, sarcastic reporters gave commentary expressing their amazement that the Amish, that anyone, could forgive the evil that had been committed that day.

How we in the church grieve and how we minister to those who grieve speaks volumes to a watching world of what this Jesus means to us. If we are the only Jesus the unsaved around us will ever see shouldn't we show them a Jesus who faces life's trials with love, hope and grace?

1 John 3:17-18 But whoso hath this world's good, and seeth his brother have need, and shutteth up his bowels of compassion from him, how dwelleth the love of God in him? My little children, let us not love in word, neither in tongue; but in deed and in truth.

I was 32 years old when my father died. He and I were very close. He was my father, my next-door neighbor and my employer, we hunted and fished together and cut wood together. We rode to church together. He was my best friend. When he died I received more comfort from an unsaved, not-very-close, friend than I did from my entire church body. This friend called me one day and expressed his concern for me and then ended the conversation with, "If you ever need anything, any time; if you ever need anyone to talk to, you call me." You know the best part? He meant it. I could have called him at three o'clock in the morning and he would have gotten together with me to talk; there was never any doubt in my mind about that.

James 2:15-16 If a brother or sister be naked, and destitute of daily food, And one of you say

*unto them, Depart in peace, be ye warmed and
filled; notwithstanding ye give them not those
things which are needful to the body; what doth
it profit?*

*Galatians 6:9-10 And let us not be weary in
well doing: for in due season we shall reap, if
we faint not. As we have therefore opportunity,
let us do good unto all men, especially unto them
who are of the household of faith.*

If we see a brother or sister in the Lord struggling
through a time of grief and we stand idly by, *"how
dwelleth the love of God"* in us? If we see them in need
and say, 'I'll be praying for you,' is that enough? Or
does God expect us to roll up our sleeves and enter
into their pain with them?

*John 13:34-35 A new commandment I give unto
you, That ye love one another; as I have loved
you, that ye also love one another. By this shall
all men know that ye are my disciples, if ye have
love one to another.*

The world won't notice our love by what we 'say'.
They will notice our love by what we 'do'.

*James 1:22 But be ye doers of the word, and not
hearers only, deceiving your own selves.*

In the Shadow of His Wings

The Scriptural imagery of being under God's wings
is a powerful one. Where could one be more safe
than under God's wing and next to His breast? David
speaks of making refuge there in the following Psalm.

*Psalms 57:1-11 To the chief Musician, Altaschith,
Michtam of David, when he fled from Saul in the
cave. Be merciful unto me, O God, be merciful
unto me: <u>for my soul trusteth in thee: yea, in the
shadow of thy wings will I make my refuge, until</u>*

these calamities be overpast. I will cry unto God most high; unto God that performeth all things for me. He shall send from heaven, and save me from the reproach of him that would swallow me up. Selah. God shall send forth his mercy and his truth. My soul is among lions: and I lie even among them that are set on fire, even the sons of men, whose teeth are spears and arrows, and their tongue a sharp sword. Be thou exalted, O God, above the heavens; let thy glory be above all the earth. They have prepared a net for my steps; my soul is bowed down: they have digged a pit before me, into the midst whereof they are fallen themselves. Selah. My heart is fixed, O God, my heart is fixed: I will sing and give praise. Awake up, my glory; awake, psaltery and harp: I myself will awake early. I will praise thee, O Lord, among the people: I will sing unto thee among the nations. For thy mercy is great unto the heavens, and thy truth unto the clouds. Be thou exalted, O God, above the heavens: let thy glory be above all the earth. (Emphasis added)

David was not in isolation from life's trials when he was under God's wing. He could not escape life with its hardships but he could find peace, comfort, joy and safety there. Even though we are to go to God's wing for refuge, friends still die, they still get cancer, still get in car accidents and their children still go prodigal. The safety for which we run to the shelter of God's wing is very real and it is spiritually very safe, but it is not always a physically safe place. Our earthly life may end but our spirit and our soul can be renewed in the shadow of His wings.

In the shadow of God's wings:

◊ Job lost all that he had there—his ten children died and he lost his health and wealth

99

◊ Moses died on Mount Nebo there—never reaching the land of Canaan

◊ Joseph spent his prison years there for a crime he did not commit—sold into slavery by his own family

◊ David hid from Saul's army there—in fear for his life

◊ Jeremiah wept there for the hardness of the Israelite's hearts

In the shadow of God's wings:

◊ Daniel spent time with the lions there—for obeying God rather than man

◊ Shadrach, Meshack and Abednego were in the fiery furnace there—for their obedience to God

◊ John the Baptist lost his head there—dying for the Lord

◊ Jesus shed tears there—in the Garden of Gethsemane

In the shadow of God's wings:

◊ Stephen was stoned to death and died there

◊ Paul lived with a thorn in the flesh there

◊ Peter died upside down on a cross there

◊ John was imprisoned there on the Isle of Patmos

What good is a refuge if people die there? *"...in the shadow of Thy wings will I make my refuge."* In the shadow of God's wings mercy is found. In the shadow of God's wings refuge is found. We place our trust in Him as refuge, *"my soul trusteth in thee."* It is not a whimsical trust of my mind, it is a deeply embedded trust from the depths of my soul. *"My heart is fixed,*

I will sing and give praise". I trust in the God of the sheltering wing, and will not fear what man can do— not because man cannot touch me there but because I trust God to only allow good into my life.

The Redeemer steps into our world and says:

◊ I will not abolish death but I will enter into it with you

◊ I will not abolish trials but I will give them purpose

◊ I will not kill all sinners, but I will give you love for them

◊ I will not set aside despair but I will give peace in its midst

◊ I will redeem that which seems unredeemable; I will bring peace and safety into the darkest day of your life.

Psalm 56:3 What time I am afraid, I will trust in Thee.

Psalm 56:11 In God I will place my trust, I will not be afraid what man can do to me.

Even though we may face difficult trials and even death in the shadow of His wings, it is the only safe place. It is the only safe place with perfect peace. It is the only place to go where we have no reason to fear.

It is not that we don't grieve because we are Christians, it is that our peace and joy overwhelm our grief. Our hope can never die because our Lord is the Living Hope. The hole in our heart may never go away but it never becomes what defines us—the God whose wings protect us does that.

There is no king saved by the multitude of an host: a mighty man is not delivered by much strength. An horse is a vain thing for safety: neither shall he deliver any by his great strength. Behold, the eye of the LORD is upon them that fear him, upon them that hope in his mercy; To deliver their soul from death, and to keep them alive in famine. Our soul waiteth for the LORD: he is our help and our shield. For our heart shall rejoice in him, because we have trusted in his holy name. Let thy mercy, O LORD, be upon us, according as we hope in thee. Psalm 33:16-22

This scripture points out the fallacy of trusting in our own strength or that of entities we would perceive as strong such as a horse or a large army. We would all have different ideas of strong places today but the truth of the Psalm stays true—only the Lord is strong enough to be a refuge for the troubled believer, only He is able to deliver a soul from death. Only He is able to be our help and our shield. We will trust in Him.

Chapter 9

Why?

Why do bad things happen to good people? Why would God cause this? If God did not cause this then why would He allow it? Why did God not see this coming? If He saw this coming why did He not stop it? Why would God do this to me and not to someone more evil? Sometimes we scream "why?" and other times we whisper it. Sometimes we never verbalize our doubt but silently live with the nagging question.

Numerous scholars have pointed out that God never answers the "why?" question in the book of Job. This is an age-old question that is continually being asked by God's people but it is one that, in the Scriptures, seldom elicits an answer from God.

After two chapters of introduction and 36 chapters of Job pouring out his heart to sympathetic but judgmental friends, God speaks. He finally responds to what Job sees as patently unfair treatment. I remember my first serious study of the book of Job. I was going through my own dark time and God was silent. I thought it might be sin in my life so I confessed every sin that I could think of. I confessed my family's sins and the sins of anyone else close to me...and yet God refused to speak.

I needed to know why the direction of my life had changed from up to down, from brightness to despair. At least I thought it was the logical question to ask and I assumed the scriptures would present a reasonable answer from the life of Job. So when I came to chapter 38 I was more than ready for God's justification for allowing Job's life to be devastated. I was sadly disappointed. I didn't feel I needed to know about the foundations of the world, about leviathans or the treasures of the snow. I already knew that God was the Creator and spoke all of creation into existence. I already knew that He was in control and that He was good. In those final chapters of Job God never answers the 'why' question, or the 'where' or the 'what' question. But God does answer the 'who' question.

God asks Job, *"Who is this that darkeneth counsel by words without knowledge?"*[49] I imagine this scene as God taking Job on a tour of creation much like visitors to the Creation Museum in Kentucky would experience. I have not been there but I have visited their website and have viewed the exhibit that demonstrates the magnanimity of creation. The tour starts with planet earth and then begins to pan out revealing more and more of creation. Earth's position in the Milky Way galaxy begins to disappear as the panorama of creation increases and galaxy after galaxy looms large and then seems to disappear as more of what God has spoken into existence fills the screen. Galaxies which are larger than the expanse of the 100,000 light years of our Milky Way galaxy seem only to be specks as the entirety of what man knows of God's creation fills the screen.

---

49   Job 38:2

Man's Insignificance

God replaces our 'why' question with the "Who?" question as He reminds Job who the Creator is. Job was filled with awe as the Lord listed off the earth, the heavens and the creatures that He had spoken into existence. It is what God intended, that Job begin to grasp that he was not the center of the universe and that a God who is able to speak all of this into existence with a single word is far more worthy of worship than Job had ever imagined. God's reply took Job through various aspects of creation from the earth and stars to snowflakes; from the massive behemoth to the intricate beauty of a peacock's feather. These three chapters (38-40) of Job are a powerful reminder to each of us of just one aspect of the magnitude of God—He is the Creator.

But there is another aspect to God's answer to the "who?" question. I live in a small town in Northern Michigan, a rather unpopulated portion of one of fifty states. Those fifty states make up one country among the 196 countries that make up this world. The twenty acres that I live on are barely a pinprick on the surface of the planet. I am one person in my county of 33,204 people, a tiny portion of the 318,860,000 that make up our United States and of the 7.3 billion people that are presently living on the planet. If I focus on my life and my family and my job and my church then I seem pretty significant (at least to me) but if I remember that I am number 4,987,998,612 of 7.3 billion then I don't register on anyone's scale of significance.

This part of God's answer to the 'who?' question is normally used to remind us of our insignificance. I don't believe that the Lord meant it in only that way. He certainly was reminding Job that the creature is not in a place to question the Creator. We are not in a place to question the One who holds all of His creation together by the word of His power. We are not in a place to question the One who knows the beginning from the end and whose ways are not our ways and whose thoughts are not our thoughts.

It is not uncommon for the grieving person to feel that kind of insignificance, forgotten by family, friends and church. Most grievous of all is that we can feel forgotten by God, an insignificant human in a vast ocean of 7.3 billion souls.

Job's Significance

There are many clues however that God is not treating Job as insignificant. First of all, God has been listening to Job and has heard every word he has spoken. In fact, Psalm 94:11[50] tells us that the Lord not only heard Job's every word but knew his every thought. (Job also speaks to the fact that God knows his every thought in chapter 42[51]). God has heard every comment Job has made and has listened to every complaint. God says to Job's friends *"For ye have not spoken of me the thing that is right, as my servant Job hath."*[52] God not only heard every word that Job spoke but He also heard every word that Job's comforters had spoken and He had weighed their truth and relevance.

God not only listened to Job but He replied. God lovingly spoke to Job the truths that would change his incorrect thinking. God is emphatic but not mean

---

50   Psalm 94:11 The Lord knoweth the thoughts of man, that they are vanity.

51   Job 42:1-2 Then Job answered the LORD, and said, I know that thou canst do every thing, and that no thought can be withholden from thee.

52   Job 42:7

or dismissive. He speaks to Job in a way that elicits Job's response *"I have heard of thee by the hearing of the ear: but now mine eye seeth thee."*[53]

Jesus reminded His listeners of the importance of each of them to their heavenly Father. Jesus spoke those words that day to each of us as well.

> *Matthew 10:29-31 Are not two sparrows sold for a farthing? and one of them shall not fall on the ground without your Father. But the very hairs of your head are all numbered. Fear ye not therefore, ye are of more value than many sparrows.*

We are so significant to God that He not only hears every word we speak and knows every thought that we think but He knows the number of hairs on our head. God loves His creation, He pronounced it 'good'. He loves the sparrows and knows when one falls from the sky, yet He says we are of *"more value than many sparrows."*

God is so intimately involved in the life of His children and with the trial they are facing that He guards every single hair on their head—not most of them, not all but one, but every single hair.

> *1 Samuel 14:45 And the people said unto Saul, Shall Jonathan die, who hath wrought this great salvation in Israel? God forbid: as the LORD liveth, there shall not one hair of his head fall to the ground; for he hath wrought with God this day. So the people rescued Jonathan, that he died not.*

God is in charge of my hairs, He numbers them and He determines how many, if any, hairs that I lose. It is not that He counts them every so often or takes note when I lose one or grow a new one—it is that He

---

53 Job 42:5

determines how many I gain or lose at any time. God does not treat man as insignificant. He knows us so intimately that He numbers our hairs. He treats us as so significant that He sent His Son to die for you and for me.

The Result

At this time in Job's story his sores still ran, the accusing words of his friends were fresh in his mind, his wife's words to "curse God and die" were not forgotten and his heart still had a hole the size of his ten dead children. And yet God's answer to Job produces worship.

God blessed Job. If seeing the Lord in a more full way than Job had ever imagined possible was not enough, God blessed him by adding back all that he had lost two-fold. God worked reconciliation in the life of Job with his friends and family. Those who mocked Job came and confessed to him their sin.

There are two answers to the 'who' question. The first answer is God, the Creator, Sustainer of the universes and all that is within them. The second answer to the question is Job, a beloved child of God; not insignificant but chosen. The challenge to Satan, *"Hast thou considered my servant Job, that there is none like him in the earth, a perfect and an upright man, one that feareth God, and escheweth evil?"*[54] is a testimony of what God knew to be true of Job. In the first two chapters and again in the closing chapter God calls Job His servant. God is not using the term servant here to signify a serf of no importance but to introduce a co-laborer in His work.

Wouldn't we all want to have the Lord be able to say of us when He wants to humble Satan, "Have

54 Job 1:8

you considered (insert your name here)?" Of all the people on the planet can you imagine having the Lord God choose you as the best of the best?

When God asks Job the "Where were you" questions, they are not meant to remind Job that he is but a pawn in the game of life, but to remind him of the difference between he and God. To remind Job that he was a part of God's creation; that he was a part of God's redemptive plan. To remind him that God was the Creator and Job was a beloved part of that creation.

God speaks to you and me today through the power of His Word. He reminds us that all that is going on in our life, good or bad, is going to be okay because He is God. We are safe. His promise to never leave us nor forsake us holds as true now as when first spoken thousands of years ago.

God doesn't use trials to teach us of our insignificance, exactly the opposite. He teaches us that even in His over-arching plan for the creation that He loves us. We are His beloved children. He is preparing a place for us. He is going to take us to live with Him in that special place forever.

Maybe I should restate that. This is personal. God has set His affection on me. I am his beloved child. He is preparing a place for me. I am going to live there with Him forevermore.

Psalm 102 is introduced to us as *"A prayer of the afflicted, when he is overwhelmed, and poureth out his complaint before the Lord."* The writer pours out his heart to God and in verse seven says *"I watch, and am as a sparrow alone upon the house top."* He did not know, or in his grief had forgotten, that God watches over each sparrow, even the ones that are alone on a house top. I know what it is like to feel insignificant, to feel as though there is no one who cares, but that is not taught in the Scriptures. Rather John reminds us to, *"Behold, what manner of love the Father hath bestowed upon us, that we should be called the sons of God:"*[55] How is it possible for us to think that we are insignificant or unimportant to God when He has lavished His love upon us and calls us His children?

What Did Job Learn?

Job learned that the Heavenly Father would bend low to speak to one of His children. He learned that God had heard his words, even the harsh ones, and still loved him. He learned that God was concerned about the grievances committed against him by his friends. He learned that God can bring blessing even out of unbelievable grief.

Job learned that in the darkest night of his grief that God continued to keep His promise to never leave nor forsake one of His children. He learned that God does not waste trials but uses them to grow His children towards Himself; to deepen the fellowship between He and us.

And as Job looks down upon us from heaven's shores he sees one of God's children after another reading the Book of Job to find comfort in their darkest nights. For thousands of years God's sons and daughters have found comfort from reading about Job and his God.

Why? Because God is good and He wants you and I to know that we are just as significant as was Job and that He knows our every thought and that not one hair will fall from our head without His knowledge.

---

55 1 John 3:1 Behold, what manner of love the Father hath bestowed upon us, that we should be called the sons of God: therefore the world knoweth us not, because it knew him not.

Job 42:1-6 Then Job answered the Lord, and said, I know that thou canst do every thing, and that no thought can be withholden from thee. Who is he that hideth counsel without knowledge? therefore have I uttered that I understood not; things too wonderful for me, which I knew not. Hear, I beseech thee, and I will speak: I will demand of thee, and declare thou unto me. I have heard of thee by the hearing of the ear: but now mine eye seeth thee. Wherefore I abhor myself, and repent in dust and ashes. (Emphasis added)

May our trials cause us to see God in a new light, in a new fullness, that we might say with Job that we have learned truths that are *"too wonderful"* for us to understand. And may we worship God as did Job.

Maybe my need to know 'why?' is no more important than was Job's. Maybe all that I need to know is "Who?" and "who?" Who is God and who am I? He is the Father and I am His beloved child.

We don't go through faith-shaking trials by accident. God allows our faith to be challenged because He has a purpose, He wants our faith to be strengthened. God wants His children to follow Him from a heart of love. He wants us compelled by grace to walk as closely to Him as possible. He allows horribly difficult trials into our lives while at the same time loving us passionately.

We *"count it all joy"* because we see God with a whole new depth of understanding. We begin to realize that He is enough for every situation we face in life. Whether we are on the mountain or in the valley, whether we are in the green pastures or surrounded by enemies, God is enough.

A Psalm of David. The LORD is my shepherd; I shall not want. He maketh me to lie down in green pastures: he leadeth me beside the still waters. He restoreth my soul: he leadeth me in the paths of righteousness for his name's sake. Yea, though I walk through the valley of the shadow of death, I will fear no evil: for thou art with me; thy rod and thy staff they comfort me. Thou preparest a table before me in the presence of mine enemies: thou anointest my head with oil; my cup runneth over. Surely goodness and mercy shall follow me all the days of my life: and I will dwell in the house of the LORD for ever. Psalm 23

Chapter 10

The Body of Christ

There is a role for the Church, the Body of Christ, to play in helping those in the throes of grief to begin to look up again. There is an essential truth that you must remember if you are a child of God—you are the church! When a brother or sister in the Lord is stricken with grief it is incumbent upon you to minister to them unless there is a scriptural reason why you should not. It is not the pastor's nor the deacon's responsibility to minister to every hurting person—that responsibility belongs to each individual member of the Body of Christ.

How should the church respond?

The Church should respond by going to the one hurting, offering compassion and prayer for however long it takes. Praying for someone from a distance is not the same as going to them to offer prayer and compassion. Some trials may last the remainder of someone's life; the Church is not going anywhere until the Lord's return so why can't we walk with that person for a lifetime? The Father calls us to walk with the suffering person until He counsels us otherwise.

The comfort we are to offer to hurting people is God's comfort, not ours (2 Corinthians 1:4). While it may be helpful to have traveled the same road as the one hurting, it is not essential. We cannot let ourselves off the hook for helping someone by saying we have never experienced the same type of grief they have.

As we give comfort it is essential that we be praying and seeking the Lord's wisdom and we must be open to receiving all that we need from Him. We have nothing else of value to give (John 15:5). The end of the trial may be in a few days, a few months or a few years or it may be forty years as with Moses. Death may put an end to grief but wherever its end is, God is there, He is enough and He is faithful and He has called His people to be there with Him ministering to those in need.

The Ministry No One Wants

The command to *"weep with them that weep"*[56] is given to all Christians. In 2 Corinthians chapter one Paul speaks more specifically to another group—those who have received comfort from God.

> *2 Corinthians 1:3-4 Blessed be God, even the Father of our Lord Jesus Christ, the Father of mercies, and the God of all comfort; Who comforteth us in all our tribulation, that we may be able to comfort them which are in any trouble, by the comfort wherewith we ourselves are comforted of God.*

Although God offers comfort to us it does not mean we receive comfort. Far too many of us go through the valley of the shadow[57] kicking and screaming. We

---

56   Romans 12:15

57   Psalm 23:4

look for any way of escape, for any crutch other than dependence upon God. We don't want the spiritual arms of Deuteronomy 32:27,[58] we want the flesh and blood arms of another human being. We want peace and comfort and for 'normal' to return.

If you have ever received comfort from God whether it be through the Scriptures, from a sermon or from the prayers of a fellow Believer you need no longer wonder if the Holy Spirit has a ministry for you. God has gifted you with His comfort for you to pass on to someone else in need. We receive the gift of comfort and along with it the ministry of comfort. In the same way that forgiven people are to forgive,[59] comforted people are to comfort.

> *1 Thessalonians 5:11 Wherefore comfort yourselves together, and edify one another, even as also ye do.*

Did you ever see some calamity befall your worst enemy? Did you wonder what to do about it? Gloating certainly isn't a viable option for a Christian and rather than gloating it may be God's plan for you to minister to your enemy—just as Jesus Christ modeled in ministering to you and me. What better way to show the grace of God than by lavishing it on our enemy? Over the years God has brought back into my life some of the people who hurt me deeply during my black years and has given me the opportunity to minister to them. It was a time of joy because it was proof that God was doing a work of healing in my life. But while I must say that it was a time of joy to

---

58 The eternal God is thy refuge, and underneath are the everlasting arms: Deuteronomy 33:27a

59 Matthew 6:14-15 For if ye forgive men their trespasses, your heavenly Father will also forgive you: But if ye forgive not men their trespasses, neither will your Father forgive your trespasses.

minister to those who had hurt me so deeply it was also a time of the Lord's testing to see if I had learned anything through the trial. I would like to say that I passed the test with flying colors but that may not be entirely accurate. But I did pass.

What Would Jesus Do?

In the 1990s a fad swept through Christian circles. WWJD or "What Would Jesus Do?" paraphernalia was everywhere. It was a good question and one that we should ask ourselves more often. Just what would Jesus do when faced with some of the trials that we face on a daily basis?

Everyone knows that *"Jesus wept."*[60] It is the favorite verse of every child who has to memorize a scripture on the spur of the moment. But Jesus' weeping at the death of a friend gives us permission to weep when we are faced with the death of someone very close to us. He is expressing His humanity and He is obeying Scripture to *"weep with them that weep."*

> *Hebrews 4:15-16 For we have not an high priest which cannot be touched with the feeling of our infirmities; but was in all points tempted like as we are, yet without sin. Let us therefore come boldly unto the throne of grace, that we may obtain mercy, and find grace to help in time of need.*

Jesus knew what it was like to be a human being. Not only had He created us, but He had lived among us with a human body, mind and spirit. He entered into Mary's and Martha's grief when He wept with them.

Jesus prayed. Throughout the Gospels we have instance after instance of Jesus getting alone to pray

---

60   John 11:35

to His Father.

> *Mark 1:35 And in the morning, rising up a great while before day, he went out, and departed into a solitary place, and there prayed.*

> *Luke 5:16 And he withdrew himself into the wilderness, and prayed.*

> *Luke 6:12 And it came to pass in those days, that he went out into a mountain to pray, and continued all night in prayer to God.*

His prayer is one of dependence. It is one of humble submission. His prayer is fervent. His prayer calls out for strength. His prayer leads to action. His prayer culminates in His sacrifice.

> *1 John 3:16-18 Hereby perceive we the love of God, because he laid down his life for us: and we ought to lay down our lives for the brethren. But whoso hath this world's good, and seeth his brother have need, and shutteth up his bowels of compassion from him, how dwelleth the love of God in him? My little children, let us not love in word, neither in tongue; but in deed and in truth.*

How can we say we have God's love in us if we see a brother or sister in the Lord in need and do nothing to help them? We dare not shut up the *"bowels of compassion"* from our brother if we have any desire to look like Jesus.

> *James 2:15-16 If a brother or sister be naked, and destitute of daily food, And one of you say unto them, Depart in peace, be ye warmed and filled; notwithstanding ye give them not those things which are needful to the body; what doth it profit?*

If we are grieving a loss we can believe that it is acceptable to weep and to mourn for the length of time God allows. We will know the acceptable length of time if we are in prayerful submission to the Father. If we are called to minister to someone who is grieving, we can pray for wisdom and take action as He leads, sacrificing ourselves to strengthen a brother or sister in the Lord.

Comfort is love expressing itself by:

◊ Patience. A broken or grieving person will not be made whole by one kind word or one pat on the back.

◊ Giving evidence of compassion. Impressing upon another that we truly do care about them, even at a time in their life when they are unlovable because of their grief.

◊ Being understanding. Sometimes grieving people will say caustic things. Sometimes they will strike out at the one trying to help them. One of the steps in their grieving is anger and it is hardly ever selective.

◊ Offering to share the burden. James warns us against offering the hungry warm platitudes without shouldering a portion of their burden.

◊ Being available. We may have to sacrifice some time and energy and we must be available on their schedule, not ours.

◊ Being wise. Men comforting someone else's wife or vice-versa can cause more trouble than it solves and in the end may be worse than no comfort at all.

What About people?

The grade we will receive on the test of our ministry to others will not be based on how many church boards we were on or how many Sunday School classes we taught. The grade will be based on what we did with people.

It is not did we teach them, but did we love them? It is not did we serve them, but did we serve them in the love of Christ? It is not how well we sang in the choir or in special numbers, but how did we allow the Holy Spirit to minister through us? It is not how well we preached, but how much did we love the people to whom we preached?

And it is not how much do we say we did all of this in love, but how did we show that love? Did the ones on the receiving end of our ministry know that we loved them? Jesus reminds us that our love must be observable *"A new commandment I give unto you, That ye love one another; as I have loved you, that ye also love one another. By this shall all men know that ye are my disciples, if ye have love one to another."*[61]

Things to Say or Things Not to Say

A lay pastor who had just presided at the funeral of a church member expressed his dissatisfaction in church the next morning with his feeble attempt at comforting the family. He said that he felt so ineffectual; he didn't have the right words to say. He felt like a fish out of water. What could he do or say that would do anything to comfort this family in their loss of husband and father? He was convinced he had failed. The widow was in church that evening and during a time of testimony took the opportunity

---

61   John 13:34-35

to publicly thank the pastor for all that he had done for them during their time of sorrow. She said, "just him being there meant so much to us."

There are many times that we just don't know what is right to say. How do you bring comfort to a young mom and dad whose child died in a car accident? All the hopes and dreams that they had as parents for that child are dashed. There will be no teenage years, no driver's license, no graduation from school, no marriage and no grandchildren. What can you say at that time that will make them look beyond the hurt that they feel and see a bright future? Nothing.

It is not always a matter of saying some profound thing, of doing something that will erase all the pain and hurt for that person. It is showing that you care. There are no words to say to a wife who has just lost her husband of fifty years that are going to fill the void or ease the lonely nights. There are no words to say to the young family whose daughter has just been killed by a drunken driver that are going to cause them to forget the hole in their heart.

The important thing is to show you care. It is easy to say phrases that sound nice but they can be just words with no meaning. We might say:

◊ Call me if you need anything at all

◊ I will pray for you

◊ I will call you and we can get together

But as good as those phrases are to say they must be followed up with action. If you are not going to do what you say you will do, then do not say them, you do much more harm than good. What you say may make you and the grieved feel warm and fuzzy at the time, but when you do not follow through it makes their grief deeper. Many people I have met with in my office have told me about the legions of family and friends that promised as they were filing past the casket that they would visit or call, and then they add, "but I haven't heard from any of them in the months or years following the funeral." They have lost a loved one and they feel abandoned by their friends and the church as well. When people express their bitterness to me following a funeral it is most often in relation to unkept promises by well-meaning friends or family.

Grieving people do not need canned answers:
◊ Count it all joy
◊ God works all things together for good
◊ God is good
◊ You'll get through this
◊ God needed him more than you did
◊ You can always have another child
◊ You can always remarry

Some of those responses are based on Scripture but it is easy to throw a portion of scripture at someone and hurry on to our destination. It is something else to sit down with them and open the Word of God, to take as much time as they need to understand that they can 'count it all joy' and God does 'work all things together for good'. These are not trite phrases, they are deep truths from the Word of God that remind us that God is in control—and He is good.

An old Black spiritual says, "Sometimes I feel like a motherless child...a long way from home." It is difficult for us to place our emptiness on a par with the black slaves who had been stolen from their family and homes, placed in the hold of a ship to be transported across the ocean, sold at an auction to the highest bidder, a man or woman never seen before, and to spend a life being sold and re-sold, worked too hard and beaten if they tried to escape. When a slave sang that song they were indeed alone although surrounded by people.

But when we have suffered some heart-breaking loss we can feel the same emptiness, "like a motherless child, a long, long way from home." We can feel just as alone in a crowded room, just as alone in an overflowing church and even more alone in an empty house.

When we promise to 'get together sometime' with a grieving person it may seem little to us but it can be huge to the one struggling with their aloneness, and it is even more disappointing when we fail to keep our promise.

Caring for the Grief-Stricken

Caring for the grieving is an inconspicuous ministry; it is done in the out-of-the-way places. Few others will know that we have given any comfort at all. 'How will we know that we have served You?' they asked. Jesus responded 'when you have done it unto the least of these.' [62]

It is easy to condemn those who seem to be mired in their grief. It is easy to run the other way when

62 Matthew 25:35-40 For I was an hungred, and ye gave me meat: I was thirsty, and ye gave me drink: I was a stranger, and ye took me in: Naked, and ye clothed me: I was sick, and ye visited me: I was in prison, and ye came unto me. Then shall the righteous answer him, saying, Lord, when saw we thee an hungred, and fed thee? or thirsty, and gave thee drink? When saw we thee a stranger, and took thee in? or naked, and clothed thee? Or when saw we thee sick, or in prison, and came unto thee? And the King shall answer and say unto them, Verily I say unto you, Inasmuch as ye have done it unto one of the least of these my brethren, ye have done it unto me.

we see them coming or to let voicemail record their phone call. But we will never know the load they are carrying if we don't listen to their words and to their heart. We cannot help carry their load if we don't know what their load is. And we will never fulfill the law of Christ[63] if we don't give of ourselves, sacrificing our time and our energy to help someone who is in the grip of grief.

> *2 Corinthians 7:5-7 For, when we were come into Macedonia, our flesh had no rest, but we were troubled on every side; without were fightings, within were fears. Nevertheless God, that comforteth those that are cast down, comforted us by the coming of Titus; And not by his coming only, but by the consolation wherewith he was comforted in you, when he told us your earnest desire, your mourning, your fervent mind toward me; so that I rejoiced the more.*

It is the Holy Spirit flowing through us that ministers to others. Some plant, some water, and it is always God that gives the increase.[64]

The Church should be a safe place for grieving people to express their grief, regardless of the reason for that grief. Grieving people should feel comfortable in sharing their pain without accusations of being weak or unspiritual. You and I are the church. You and I are the ones who must patiently listen. You and I are the ones who must listen to their heart, not just their words, and we must listen to the Holy Spirit's prompting for what to say or not to say back to them. You and I are the ones who need to be ready with scripture to respond to their troubled soul. You and

---

63 Galatians 6:2 Bear ye one another's burdens, and so fulfil the law of Christ.

64 1 Corinthians 3:6

I must be willing to sacrifice our time to strengthen a brother or sister in the Lord.

I usually am able to speak to people who come to my office in a way that offers some comfort or at least some relief from their immediate cares. One summer I met with the family of a middle-aged husband and father who had committed suicide. Regardless of what I tried to say to his family my words were met with resistance. I met with them again a few days later with the same results. A few months later I was able to minister to the wife and mother with some effectiveness. In that time the Lord prepared her and me for the words that He wanted me to say. I did not give up even though I had been rebuffed the first few times.

This experience reminded me that I have nothing to say to grieving people. It is only through the Lord's prompting and through His ministry that I have anything to say. Our purpose is to show them Jesus; it is to show them that Someone cares for them and desires to comfort their heaviest burdens.

Long Term Grief—Long Term Care

Mark and Debbie have a special needs child. Mary is an energetic, bright young girl, presently in the fifth grade. Debbie wrote on Facebook of an upcoming conference aimed at helping people communicate with her daughter. Debbie added: "I am thankful there are so many people in Mary's life who care enough to come to a communication conference but very sad and emotional we have to do it at all. I want to be watching her play volleyball not teaching her how to communicate."

Mark and Debbie are in their late forties and are facing a lifetime of care for their daughter. Most parents their age are preparing their children for college, for marriage or for a career. Mark and Debbie will never in this lifetime know a day when their daughter will be able to live without someone's care.

How do we minister to Mark and Debbie and to Mary? Do we say "into every life a little rain must fall?" Do we sympathize for a few days, weeks or months? Or do we offer them a night out every so often while we watch Mary? Do we take Mary out to eat at her favorite restaurant so Mark and Debbie can be alone for a few hours?

It is easy to bring lasagna to the house for a week or two after a death or a terminal diagnosis but it is something else to bring lasagna every week for two years...or for ten years. How do we minister to those with life-long trials, or do we think that after a couple months they have assimilated their new lifestyle and moved on with their journey?

It is generally accepted that recovering from the death of a spouse will take two years. Some grieving persons may take more, a few may take less. But do we minister to the grieving for all of those two years or more? Should we?

Most of the people I meet are not looking for a continual 'fuss' to be made over them but they do appreciate it when someone notices their loss; when someone says they are praying for them, when someone offers kind words. Or when someone acknowledges their faithfulness to church even though they face hardships in getting there that most of us never know.

Thy mercy, O LORD, is in the heavens; and thy faithfulness reacheth unto the clouds. Thy righteousness is like the great mountains; thy judgments are a great deep: O LORD, thou preservest man and beast. How excellent is thy lovingkindness, O God! therefore the children of men put their trust under the shadow of thy wings. They shall be abundantly satisfied with the fatness of thy house; and thou shalt make them drink of the river of thy pleasures. For with thee is the fountain of life: in thy light shall we see light. O continue thy lovingkindness unto them that know thee; and thy righteousness to the upright in heart. Psalm 36:5-10

Chapter 11

What Will You Choose?

A passage of Scripture that always amazes me is the story of the rich young ruler.[65] Jesus gave him opportunity to follow Him with only one requirement— that he sell all that he owned. When the young man could not do that Jesus let him walk away. It was his choice whether he would follow Jesus or not. Jesus did not run after him nor did He did change the terms of the cost of following. He still gives us choices today. Will we follow Him or that which seems best to us?[66]

Many of the people whose grieving I had listed previously I either know personally or have followed their lives as best I am able. Some of them have grown in the Lord because of their trials while others have turned bitter and have turned away from Him. One man told me that if his father who had just passed away was in hell (he was as sure as any of us can be that is where his father was) then he wanted to go to hell too. This man claimed to be a Christian, he

---

65 Matthew 19:16-30

66 Proverbs 14:12 There is a way which seemeth right unto a man, but the end thereof are the ways of death.

knew what the Bible has to say about hell and yet he wanted to be with his dad rather than with his Savior. I don't think he would say those words these many years later but he has grown very little in the Lord since then. That was his choice.

Another man whose young son had died in a tragic accident, told me that he kept a journal of his good days and his bad days. He wrote everything down, recording the work that the Lord was doing in his life. He said he was afraid that if he did not keep a record for future reference that he would "waste the journey." Is there a hole in his heart caused by the death of his son? Absolutely. Many years later he still sheds tears when talking about him. Has he grown in the Lord in spite of (or because of) the hole in his heart? Absolutely. That was his choice.

> *Romans 8:28-30 And we know that all things work together for good to them that love God, to them who are the called according to his purpose. For whom he did foreknow, he also did predestinate to be conformed to the image of his Son, that he might be the firstborn among many brethren. Moreover whom he did predestinate, them he also called: and whom he called, them he also justified: and whom he justified, them he also glorified.*

Paul says that we can know without a shadow of a doubt that God works *"all things"* together for good for them who are the called. He did not say 'some of the things' or 'most things' or 'every so often something good works out.' He said *"all things."* And God allows even hard things to come into our life so we might be *"conformed to the image of his Son."*

Jacob's son Joseph had many reasons to grieve. He lost his home, his fellowship with his father and family and he was sold into slavery by those who were supposed to love him. He was thrown into prison for being godly and he was forgotten by a fellow prisoner whom he had helped. Later, when he was able to confront his brothers who had waffled between killing him or selling him into slavery he did the unimaginable; he forgave them.

> *Genesis 50:19-21 And Joseph said unto them, Fear not: for am I in the place of God? But as for you, ye thought evil against me; but God meant it unto good, to bring to pass, as it is this day, to save much people alive. Now therefore fear ye not: I will nourish you, and your little ones. And he comforted them, and spake kindly unto them.*

Joseph realized that God was in control of his entire life. Scripture records that it was God who sent Joseph to Egypt. Joseph knew something else that is crucially important to the life of every believer. He knew that God is in control and He is also good.

> *Psalm 105:16-17 Moreover he [God] called for a famine upon the land: he [God] brake the whole staff of bread. He [God] sent a man before them, even Joseph, who was sold for a servant: Emphasis added.*

All of the trials Joseph had faced had not turned him into a bitter, scheming, angry man who was just waiting for the opportunity to punish his brothers for what they had done to him. Rather he saw that *"God meant it unto good...to save much people alive."* That was his choice.

God has a purpose in your trial and in your grief. It is to conform you to His image. We live in a fallen world where sin, disease and death affect us all. Yet even in all of that God is able to work good. The question for us is not whether God can work good, but will we know His good when we see it? Does God have to give us what we want, the way we want it, in order for us to love Him?

If we live long enough grief will be no stranger. A friend will die in an automobile accident, a family member will be stricken with cancer and die, a beloved friend will walk off into the netherworld of Alzheimer's and someday we will face our own mortality.

Grief is not uncommon nor is it un-Christian. But how we face our grief can be un-Christian; it can be sin. It is to us, as believers then, to grieve in a way honoring to the Lord and for as long as He knows is best. For some, as our friend whose son died 33 years ago, that grief will last an entire lifetime, but it should not cripple our fellowship with the Lord nor should it define us. For others, who are grieving the loss of the best job they ever had, there will be a time when they should begin to see the good that God is working—and rather than grieve the loss of the job *"count it all joy"* that growing in the *"grace and knowledge of our Lord and Saviour Jesus Christ"*[67] is far better than any job could ever be. The loss that we face should never overwhelm us to the point where we cannot rejoice in the Lord.

> When life is rosy, we may slide by with knowing about Jesus, with imitating him and quoting him and speaking of him. But only in the fellowship of suffering will we know Jesus. We identify with him at the point of his deepest humiliation. The cross, symbol of his greatest suffering, becomes our personal touch-point with the Lord of the universe.
>
> Joni Eareckson Tada

---

67 2 Peter 3:18 But grow in grace, and in the knowledge of our Lord and Saviour Jesus Christ. To him be glory both now and for ever. Amen.

What Will We Choose?

When we make the choice to serve the Lord we give up the choice to serve self. If we choose God's Word and we choose to delight in Him and to delight in His Word; if we meditate on His Word, allowing it to govern our day—then our life will be blessed. It is our choice. We can choose self or walking with God, one or the other, but we cannot choose both.

George, whose son died in his early 20s, said, "we deal with the death of our son with gracious anguish." There is no anguish that God cannot cover with His grace—not the death of a child nor the death of a spouse. God's grace is great enough for any trial we may face. Even though with some trials a scar may remain as long as we live on this earth, God's grace is sufficient even in that.

We choose to become harder or softer; we choose to become more judgmental or more gracious; we choose to become more ungodly or more like Christ. God allows us to face life-changing trials for our good, to reveal our true character and to cause our character to line up with His. We can walk away from or towards the Lord—it is our choice.

My niece wrote the following words following the premature birth and premature death of her granddaughter, Gracelyn Marie.

> My "word" for 2016 is TRUST. So many
> reasons this week to trust. So many
> crossroads where I had to choose fear
> or trust. I did not always succeed, and
> moments of fear and anxiety moved in.
> But God, who is so gracious moved in
> larger, more fully, more magnificently
> than I could ever have imagined. Trusting

through the scary times, trusting through the heartache, trusting amidst the tears of loss, trusting through the grief. And I can truly say, "It is well with my soul." This peace I feel is not of this world. This peace is straight from my heavenly Father, the God of all comfort, the One who says, "Come to me and I will give you rest." The One who, "... holds all my tears in a bottle." The One who is my Refuge and shelters me, "... in the shadow of His wings." The One who, "...rides across the skies to help me." And in the end, I simply trust. Trust that He is a Good, Good Father. Trust that ALL His ways are perfect. Trust that He will NEVER leave me or forsake me. Trust that He has GOOD plans. Gracelyn Marie, thank you for teaching me to trust my God more fully. Your little life, no matter how brief, has touched our lives in significant ways. And I TRUST that one day I will hold you in my arms again.

Sometimes we trust the Lord with a puffed out chest and a defiant tone and other times we trust Him through tear-stained eyes and a broken heart— but we trust. Her words are filled with Scripture, the safest place to run when we need to be reminded of the promises that the faithful God not only makes but keeps.

Knowing who God was in the past helps us to know who He is in our present. Reading the Old Testament with its stories of crossing the Red Sea on dry ground, the walls of Jericho falling in and the never-ending supply of oil and grain for the widow of Zerephath should give us confidence in the God who has promised to strengthen us.

> *2 Corinthians 4:8-11 We are troubled on every side, yet not distressed; we are perplexed, but not in despair; Persecuted, but not forsaken; cast down, but not destroyed; Always bearing about in the body the dying of the Lord Jesus, that the life also of Jesus might be made manifest in our body. For we which live are alway delivered unto death for Jesus' sake, that the life also of Jesus might be made manifest in our mortal flesh.*

> *2 Corinthians 4:16-18 For which cause we faint not; but though our outward man perish, yet the inward man is renewed day by day. For our light affliction, which is but for a moment, worketh for us a far more exceeding and eternal weight of glory; While we look not at the things which are seen, but at the things which are not seen: for the things which are seen are temporal; but the things which are not seen are eternal.*

God ministers to me using different people and different scriptures than He might use to minister to you. I have shared my favorite passages of scripture with others thinking that they would mean as much to them as they did to me—they did not. I have told some how God has worked in my life and they have been greatly helped and I have told the same stories to others who have received no comfort at all. It is not my words nor is it my story that gives hope and comfort and changes lives—it is the Holy Spirit, the true Comforter who does that. In order to minister to others we must be sensitive to the Holy Spirit and trust in Him for the right words and the right scriptures for each person to whom He calls us to minister. It is our choice to do so—or not.

Ministering to the Broken

The opportunities to minister may not be blatantly obvious. If we truly desire to minister to the hurting we must keep our spiritual eyes open. In Luke 8, Jesus was in a crowd of people on His way to heal Jairus' daughter when a woman in need touched the hem of His garment.[68] He could have ignored her and kept walking and only He and the woman would have known—but He stopped to minister to her. It is left to us to have that same sensitivity to the needs of others, to be sensitive to the Holy Spirit's leading us to reach out to some broken person—in need of His mending.

My parents had been married for almost 50 years. They were married the year the Great Depression began, raised four children, suffered two miscarriages and faced all the ups and downs that families face in the course of a lifetime. On July 4, 1929 they became 'one flesh' and grew together for all those years. When my dad went into the hospital on March 7, 1979, he went in as 'one flesh' with my mom but when my mom came back to the house they had shared together since 1945 she came back as 'one-half flesh.' Her other half was on a slab in a hospital morgue.

Any problems in their marriage would go unsolved. Any harsh words would go unforgiven. Any joys in their marriage would never be experienced

---

68 Luke 8:43-46 And a woman having an issue of blood twelve years, which had spent all her living upon physicians, neither could be healed of any, Came behind him, and touched the border of his garment: and immediately her issue of blood stanched. And Jesus said, Who touched me? When all denied, Peter and they that were with him said, Master, the multitude throng thee and press thee, and sayest thou, Who touched me? And Jesus said, Somebody hath touched me: for I perceive that virtue is gone out of me.

again. A kind word from the one who knew her best would never be heard again. The opportunity for a hug or a kiss from the one she loved the most was gone. The ability to share a concern or get some advice from her 'better half' was no longer an option.

The grieving people listed throughout this study are actual people who have experienced actual situations. Minister carefully to them. When you see a new widow in church you can easily throw out a few spiritual-sounding phrases and continue on your way. She will go home from church to cook a meal for one; spend an evening alone in front of the TV and fall asleep in her chair because she doesn't want to go to bed alone for the first time in many years. Your warm platitudes will mean little to her in the numbing aloneness she feels.

A lady was in my office whose 17 year-old daughter had died in a car accident 17 years previously. She told me that she 'could still cry at any time.' Because I had sold them the cemetery lot for their daughter and had other contact with them since that time, I felt comfortable in questioning her a little. She told me that she was doing well and that her grief was not morbid but that it was always present. As we talked about her daughter she beamed with pride; told funny stories and shed a few tears. We talked about what her 34 year-old daughter would be doing had she lived. As she left my office she thanked me for the time spent talking about her daughter; she said it was like being back in therapy. She meant that in a good way.

One family whose son died in a boating accident told me that some friends have sent them a sympathy card every week for the past four years. They have cared enough to spend the money for a card and postage 52 weeks a year for four years now. These friends told the grieving parents that they send the cards, "just so you will know that somebody loves you and is thinking of you." Maybe we can't send a sympathy card every week but we can make a phone call or some other effort to remind grieving people that they are loved and not forgotten.

Those who are willing to minister to the grieving must keep their hearts open for God-appointed opportunities. You may wonder if you will have the strength to help anyone else but God will not bring into your life those whom He will not strengthen you to help. We also must have discernment to listen to the Lord for those He has called us to help.

What Will You Choose?

John and Marilyn Wiles[69] are proud parents of three children. Their children became born-again Christians at an early age and matured spiritually into early adulthood. One day, while the three young adults were on their way to volunteer at a soup kitchen, their van was struck broadside by a driver distracted while talking on his cell phone. Their children were all killed instantly. The driver of the other car, the one who was distracted by his phone, walked away from the accident unscathed and unashamed.

'Surely goodness and mercy will follow you Marilyn, all the days of your life'.[70] Her faith is staggered; it wavers for more than a few months as she sorts through the onrushing torrent of emotions. The stages of grief are pronounced as she lingers on

---

69 This is a fictional story but it is similar to stories many of us know.

70 Psalms 23:6 Surely goodness and mercy shall follow me all the days of my life: and I will dwell in the house of the LORD for ever.

each one: denial, guilt, anger...they are checked off, one by one, as Marilyn experiences their dreadful fullness. Eventually she is able to see God's hand at work in her life, and she begins a ministry with the hospital chaplain to people facing tragedies of their own. There will always be a hole in her heart and reminders of what could have been, but she gives the rest of her life, including the hole, to God for His use. She knows that her children, and God, would want her to help others and not go into a shell from which she would never come out.

'Surely goodness and mercy will follow you John, all the days of your life.' His faith is knocked down and out for the count, never to get back up again. He is like a sucker-punched boxer, he can breathe in but not out. He can't pray. Why bother? What good does it do? He had prayed for his children the very day of the accident—and God let them die. He can't read the Bible without choking on the promises God makes but doesn't seem to keep. What kind of God would cause, or at best allow, such an accident? John dies 11 years later, a shell of a man. For all practical purposes he died the day that fateful cell phone call claimed the lives of his children. He made it through the denial phase of the grieving process, he was well aware that this tragedy had happened to Him. He never did move beyond the anger phase however—anger towards the driver of the other car, anger towards the lawmakers that refuse to pass a law against talking on the phone while driving, anger with his former wife for moving on with her life, anger with his children for being together that day, anger at soup kitchens...but mainly anger at God, the One that says He is good and merciful but, in John's mind, doesn't deliver. He just doesn't need that kind of 'goodness.' Not anymore.

Does God's goodness and mercy only follow some people, in this case Marilyn, but not John? Does God only make promises to some of His children—but not all of them? Does He make promises because it feels good to make them but He really lacks what it takes to keep them?

The promise is definite. 'Surely goodness and mercy will follow you all the days of your life.' The promise is specific, it is personal and it is forever. But why do some find goodness and mercy following them while others grow bitter and see no signs of goodness or experience even a hint of mercy?

The just shall live by faith. Faith that God keeps all of His promises, all of the time. What changed in Job's life when he repented in sackcloth and ashes? Only his faith in God. His health hadn't changed, his children were still dead, his wealth was still lost and there is no mention made of his wife supporting him. Yet Job speaks with conviction of his satisfaction in knowing God. Had goodness and mercy really been following Him all the time, even during those interminable days in the middle of his story when his anger overflowed? The answer is a resounding yes.

Chapter 12

Conclusion

You can take all the courses on grieving available to you. You can check off every box on the best lists of how to recover from grief. You can study Scripture and pray. You can seek wise counsel from other believers. But Jesus' question to the man at the Pool of Bethesda haunts us all, 'Do YOU want to be made whole?' It is a question we must ask ourselves. Do you want to be made well, even if that means you have to say goodbye to your life as you knew it? Are you willing to trust God that He is able to work good— even in what seems to be the worst days of your life?

It has been mentioned numerous times in this study that those who have been comforted are called to give comfort to hurting people. It is a choice we make in obedience to minister or in disobedience to sit on the sidelines. There should be little question in anyone's mind as to where God's blessing will be found.

The Choice to Minister

Some friends of ours lived in a small town. They seemed to be the ideal couple. He was a part-time pastor and mailman; she was a loving housewife, mother and grandmother. They were only a couple of years from retirement when she, in her early 50's, began showing the signs of Alzheimer's. It wasn't long before she was in the throes of the dreaded disease. Her husband vowed to care for her at home as long as he could but the time came when he could no longer care for her needs by himself and was forced to put her in a care home that specialized in caring for those with dementia.

I can only imagine the emotions that raged within him as he drove home from the care home that first day...fear and anger, grief, a sense of aloneness and the feeling that he had failed to keep his promise. But he was true to his word; he continued to care for her, going to the nursing home twice a day to help with her every need. He would feed her and help clean her and try to comfort her. Day after day, for years, as he cared for her he also cared for the staff and their special needs. He pastored a little flock there in that nursing home. He gave cups of water in Jesus' name, setting an example for other believers to follow and showing the world a little example of Christ's faithfulness to His people. There are people in that town who have a little different view of Christians and Christ today than they had ten years ago because of one man's commitment and faithfulness.

Christ's light shone through the cracked earthenware vessel of that faithful husband into a world that needs to see the power—and grace—of the Lord.

How can the world see that we have an unshakable faith? Is it because of the teachings of the health and wealth preachers that tell us if we give enough to their ministry that God will bless us with a

Cadillac and a new home? Or is it as the world sees the Body being the Body of Christ that He intended us to be? Will they will see our faith as they see His light shining forth from some very worn, very cracked, but faithful vessels? It is our choice.

Doubt sees the obstacles.
Faith sees the way!
Doubt sees the darkest night,
Faith sees the day!
Doubt dreads to take a step.
Faith soars on high!
Doubt questions, "Who believes?"
Faith answers, "I!"

Gospel Banner. Tan, P. L. (1996). Encyclopedia of 7700 Illustrations: Signs of the Times (p. 404). Garland, TX: Bible Communications, Inc.

Daniel 3:16-18 Shadrach, Meshach, and Abednego, answered and said to the king, O Nebuchadnezzar, we are not careful to answer thee in this matter. If it be so, our God whom we serve is able to deliver us from the burning fiery furnace, and he will deliver us out of thine hand, O king. But if not, be it known unto thee, O king, that we will not serve thy gods, nor worship the golden image which thou hast set up.

Daniel 3:27-28 And the princes, governors, and captains, and the king's counsellors, being gathered together, saw these men, upon whose bodies the fire had no power, nor was an hair of their head singed, neither were their coats changed, nor the smell of fire had passed on them. Then Nebuchadnezzar spake, and said, Blessed be the God of Shadrach, Meshach, and Abednego, who hath sent his angel, and delivered his servants that trusted in him, and have changed the king's word, and yielded their bodies, that they might not serve nor worship any god, except their own God.

Appendix

The Prayer Meeting

I have included this story I wrote many years ago because it speaks to how we normally pray and how God sometimes answers. No one would pray for the trial that Job went through but the Lord used that in Job's life to bless him and He has been using Job's story to strengthen His people down through the ages. May this little story help to remind us of *"the depth of the riches both of the wisdom and knowledge of God! how unsearchable are his judgments, and his ways past finding out!"*[71]

It is a November Wednesday evening in a small country Baptist church in Northern Michigan. With only a few weeks until Thanksgiving the short teaching service is centered around the blessings of God. The pastor shares his desire to see additional members join the

---

71 Romans 11:33 O the depth of the riches both of the wisdom and knowledge of God! how unsearchable are his judgments, and his ways past finding out!

church and to have increased giving in order to begin work on a handicap ramp for better access to the auditorium. He then asks the people to share their prayer requests.

The small church stays together to pray this evening. Normally they split up into smaller groups but there are not that many folks out tonight and the Thanksgiving season is family time. Everyone is encouraged to pray and some of the little ones express their gratitude for a long break from school or the anticipation of a large meal. Older folk pray for health concerns and some pray for Aunt Jennie, one of the faithful members of the church who is now in a care home. Most everyone prays for "travelling mercies" for the ones traveling on the highways at holiday time. It is a fairly typical Wednesday evening prayer meeting.

Then Ed begins to pray, in a way that the members have never heard him pray previously. His voice trembles as he begins, "My Father, You know that I have been blessed beyond measure. My wife and our children and their families have farmland, and dairy cattle, and buildings, and financial resources more than we ever thought we would have. You know that I have been thankful for those blessings and have been able to give back to the church. But tonight, dear Lord, I humbly pray that You will bless our family by killing every animal that we own. And Lord, You know how much my wife and I love our family, but I pray that as our children gather together for Thanksgiving dinner that You will bless us by causing each one of them to die. It will be hard to lose them but I know that we will see them again someday. Father, one of the reasons I have been able to amass such a great fortune is because of my physical health, and I pray right now that Your blessing for me will be to take away that health. I need to suffer some, Lord, and I thank You in advance for the opportunity to do so. And if it is not asking too much, could I ask You for one more blessing—to have my wife and my friends reject me, leaving me with no friend in this world? Lord, you have taught me how to live with abundance, now will You bless me by teaching me how to live with nothing and no one...except You? Thank you, Lord. In Thy name I pray, Amen."[72]

The pastor didn't know how to respond. Bible college and seminary had not trained him how to handle a prayer like that. Was he supposed to wait for someone else to pray? Was he to close the service quickly and begin preparing a sermon for Sunday explaining why Ed is no longer in the church? But he was too slow to make a decision. It was John's turn to pray.

John was a young man, part of a good family in the church. He showed great potential and he was his dad's favorite—a fact that didn't set well with his siblings. John's prayer began in a quiet whisper, barely audible to those in the back, "Father, after hearing Brother Ed pray I have realized that I have been praying for wrong things. I have been praying for 'stuff' for me. Tonight Lord, I want to pray for Your blessings as I never have before. Father, I pray that my family's jealousy will come to a head and that my siblings will sell me into a foreign slave market where I will know no one and there will be no other Christians. I pray Lord that if I am blessed enough to get a job there that You will see to it that I am lied about for trying to honor You and that I get thrown into prison. I pray Lord for You to bless me by having fellow prisoners that I thought were my friends forget

72 See the Book of Job, chapters one and two

me when they have the chance to help me. I ask Your forgiveness Lord for always praying for good health and a college scholarship. I pray tonight for the blessing of prison instead. Thank you Lord, for hearing my prayer. I hope I haven't asked for too much. Amen." [73]

The pastor still didn't know what to do. Should he jump to his feet and close the service; thanking the Lord for the work He had done in their midst that evening? Should he ask Brian to close in prayer? Brian is always trustworthy to pray a 'normal' prayer, one that asks for physical healing, safe driving and generic blessings followed by a quick "Amen."

Instead, without thinking, the young pastor began to pray. "Lord, I have been asking You for a wife to bless me in my ministry. Tonight Lord, I am thanking You for the blessing of singleness, so I can give myself to the work of Your ministry. I have been asking Lord that You would heal my headaches that keep me from studying the way I would like to. I have asked You three times for healing. But now Lord, I am going to "count it all joy" that You have given me this affliction. I can see how these headaches keep me from being prideful and help me to focus on my need of You. Thank You Lord, for the blessing of migraines. Before tonight Lord, I had my plans laid out in front of me. Now Lord, I throw my plans away and I humbly pray that more than anything in the world, You will help me to really know You. I want Your power to flow though my life and I promise not to take any of the credit for the work Your power accomplishes. I pray Lord that I can partake of Your sufferings, help me Lord to "fellowship" with You in that way. And finally

---

73   See Joseph's story in the Book of Genesis

Lord, may my life and my death, be just like Your life and Your death—in total submission to the Father. I know these are a lot of blessings to ask for Lord, but I ask humbly and with a pure heart. Please understand Lord that I don't want to be greedy. Amen." [74]

The service closed without any other words being said but few left the auditorium. Those who stayed were silent, afraid to pray and afraid not to. They felt like they were in a holy place and didn't want to leave.

Romans 8:26 says that *"we know not what we should pray for"* but maybe it is because we never prayed as Ed and John and the young pastor prayed. Maybe we are afraid that the Lord might actually answer that type of prayer and bless us in the same way He blessed Job and Joseph and the Apostle Paul. And maybe, if we prayed that prayer, we would never be the same again. And just maybe that is what makes us afraid to pray it.

I am sure that Job didn't pray for the loss of all that he had and all that he was—but he thanked God for the blessing afterwards. He thanked God for the blessing of being able to *"see Him"* when it seemed as though before he had only heard of God.

> *Job 42:1-6 Then Job answered the Lord, and said, I know that thou canst do every thing, and that no thought can be withholden from thee. Who is he that hideth counsel without knowledge? therefore have I uttered that I understood not; things too wonderful for me, which I knew not. Hear, I beseech thee, and I will speak: I will demand of thee, and declare thou unto me. I have heard of thee by the hearing of the ear: but now mine eye seeth thee. Wherefore I abhor myself, and repent in dust and ashes.*

---

74 See the Apostle Paul's story in the Book of 2 Corinthians

I can't imagine young Joseph praying for prison for seeking to honor God – but He saw that God used it all for good, in his own life, in his family's lives and in the Nation of Israel.

> *Genesis 50:19-20 And Joseph said unto them, Fear not: for am I in the place of God? But as for you, ye thought evil against me; but God meant it unto good, to bring to pass, as it is this day, to save much people alive.*

And Paul prayed to have the thorn removed—until He realized that there were far more blessings in the thorn than in its absence.

> *2 Corinthians 12:8-10 For this thing I besought the Lord thrice, that it might depart from me. And he said unto me, My grace is sufficient for thee: for my strength is made perfect in weakness. Most gladly therefore will I rather glory in my infirmities, that the power of Christ may rest upon me. Therefore I take pleasure in infirmities, in reproaches, in necessities, in persecutions, in distresses for Christ's sake: for when I am weak, then am I strong.*

Each of the men found that knowing God intimately is far better than health or wealth or safe driving or any "blessing" man is prone to ask for.

> *Romans 8:26, 28-29 Likewise the Spirit also helpeth our infirmities: for we know not what we should pray for as we ought: but the Spirit itself maketh intercession for us with groanings which cannot be uttered. And we know that all things work together for good to them that love God, to them who are the called according to his purpose. For whom he did foreknow, he also did predestinate to be conformed to the image of his Son, that he might be the firstborn among many brethren.*

I would never suggest that we pray like the men in these stories. The church could not honor a man who would pray for his children to be killed. The police or social workers would be called if a young father prayed such a prayer. Counseling would be offered to someone who prayed that he would be thrown into prison.

What I am suggesting is that we don't know how to pray. Who would ever pray for their siblings to mistreat them? For friends to forget them? For prison time? Any of us would feel wrong to ask the Lord for such things, yet those are exactly the "blessings" that the Lord poured out on Job and Joseph and Paul.

I am suggesting that many times we ask for wrong things; for trivial things. I am suggesting that we don't know what "blessing" from the hand of God looks like. What blessing does my heart long for? For God to touch me in such a way that I am forever changed to look more like Him...or for things that I 'may consume on my lusts?' Sometimes the Lord blesses the weak with strength, but sometimes He blesses the strong with weakness. Sometimes He blesses the poor with wealth, yet other times He blesses the rich with poverty.

When we pray, if the Holy Spirit sees that our heart is tender towards the Father, and that the passion of our life is to serve Him, and we desire more than anything to look like Jesus, He just might intercede on our behalf with the Father and bless us like He did Job and Joseph and Paul. Blessing us with knowing Him in a far more intimate way than we had ever imagined.

I pray that the Lord can accomplish that in my life. I pray that I don't need to experience the loss of all that I have and all that I am to be able to receive this kind of blessing from His gracious hand. I pray that the Holy Spirit will understand from my humble words that I want to *"know him, and the power of his resurrection, and the fellowship of his sufferings, being made conformable unto his death." (Philippians 3:10)* And most of all, I pray that I want that more than I want anything else.

Seven Stages of Grief

1. Shock And Denial [75]

You will probably react to learning of the loss with numbed disbelief. You may deny the reality of the loss at some level, in order to avoid the pain. Shock provides emotional protection from being overwhelmed all at once. This may last for weeks.

2. Pain And Guilt

As the shock wears off, it is replaced with the suffering of unbelievable pain. Although excruciating and almost unbearable, it is important that you experience the pain fully, and not hide it, avoid it or escape from it with alcohol or drugs.

You may have guilty feelings or remorse over things you did or didn't do with your loved one. Life feels chaotic and scary during this phase.

3. Anger And Bargaining

Frustration gives way to anger, and you may lash out and lay unwarranted blame for the death on someone else. Please try to control this, as permanent damage

---

75   Taken from www.Recover-from-grief.com

to your relationships may result. This is a time for the release of bottled up emotion.

You may rail against fate, questioning "Why me?" You may also try to bargain in vain with the powers that be for a way out of your despair ("I will never drink again if you just bring him back")

4. Depression, Reflection, Loneliness

Just when your friends may think you should be getting on with your life, a long period of sad reflection will likely overtake you . This is a normal stage of grief, so do not be "talked out of it" by well-meaning outsiders. Encouragement from others is not helpful to you during this stage of grieving.

During this time, you finally realize the true magnitude of your loss, and it depresses you. You may isolate yourself on purpose, reflect on things you did with your lost one, and focus on memories of the past. You may sense feelings of emptiness or despair.

5. The Upward Turn

As you start to adjust to life without your dear one, your life becomes a little calmer and more organized. Your physical symptoms lessen, and your "depression" begins to lift slightly.

6. Reconstruction And Working Through

As you become more functional, your mind starts working again, and you will find yourself seeking realistic solutions to problems posed by life without your loved one. You will start to work on practical and financial problems and reconstructing yourself and your life without him or her.

7. Acceptance And Hope

During this, the last of the seven stages in this grief model, you learn to accept and deal with the reality of your situation. Acceptance does not necessarily mean instant happiness. Given the pain and turmoil you have experienced, you can never return to the carefree, untroubled YOU that existed before this tragedy. But you will find a way forward.

You will start to look forward and actually plan things for the future. Eventually, you will be able to think about your lost loved one without pain; sadness, yes, but the wrenching pain will be gone. You will once again anticipate some good times to come, and yes, even find joy again in the experience of living.

Hope Dies After A Long Illness

Hope died today at age 57. It was birthed in a tiny heart in a hospital delivery room what seems like a decade or more ago now. Hope was strong in the early years and had a promising future but a childhood of emotional abuse by uncaring parents caused the once vital force to slowly erode in stature. A lost job, a failed marriage, the death of a childhood friend all did their part to keep hope from blooming in this once confident life.

Hope had no children but its weakened condition gave birth to two stepchildren: bitterness and despair.

Hope suffered a long, lingering, lonely death. Hope's siblings, faith and love had been disinherited, pushed aside by the long sickness that had permeated the soul, leaving no room for loving relationships of any kind.

There will be no visitation because no vestige of hope remains to be viewed.

There will be no funeral services for hope—only for the life it once gave meaning to. Hope's death caused a void in many lives, a hole that can only be filled by the Living Hope—Jesus Christ. But that takes faith... and love. KC

Seven Responses to Grief

1. Pray

It is not uncommon to hear people say, "I came to the point where all I could do was pray." That is exactly where God wants us to be.

> "I have been driven many times to my knees by the overwhelming conviction that I had nowhere to go. My own wisdom, and that of all about me, seemed insufficient for the day." Abraham Lincoln

> Martin Luther, when once asked what his plans for the following day were answered: "Work, work, from early until late. In fact, I have so much to do that I shall spend the first three hours in prayer."

Jesus set a pattern for us by praying to His Father every morning, in the Garden and in the Upper Room. He taught us how to pray in the Sermon on the Mount.

Paul teaches us to *"pray without ceasing"*[76] and it

---

76   1 Thessalonians 5:17 Pray without ceasing

makes no sense to stop praying when life is hard and we are in the throes of grief.

2. Study the Word, Know What You Know

There are plenty of helpful books, sermons, group sessions, and counselors who will help you with your grief. But you must be careful to choose the ones who point you to the God through the Scriptures.

What in the Word of God do you know for sure, beyond any shadow of doubt? The Psalmist of Psalm 46 tells us to *"Be still, and know that I am God."*[77] We can be still because of what we know to be true from God's Word.

3. Trust

God is faithful.[78] If we can trust Him with our eternity, we certainly can trust Him with our days here, even the most difficult of days.

> *Psalm 5:11 But let all those that put their trust in thee rejoice: let them ever shout for joy, because thou defendest them: let them also that love thy name be joyful in thee.*
>
> *Psalm 56:3-4 What time I am afraid, I will trust in thee. In God I will praise his word, in God I have put my trust; I will not fear what flesh can do unto me.*
>
> *Psalm 92:2 I will say of the LORD, He is my refuge and my fortress: my God; in him will I trust.*
>
> *Psalm 20:5-8 We will rejoice in thy salvation,*

---

77   Psalm 46:10

78   2 Thessalonians 3:3   But the Lord is faithful, who shall stablish you, and keep you from evil.

and in the name of our God we will set up our banners: the LORD fulfil all thy petitions. Now know I that the LORD saveth his anointed; he will hear him from his holy heaven with the saving strength of his right hand. Some trust in chariots, and some in horses: but we will remember the name of the LORD our God. They are brought down and fallen: but we are risen, and stand upright.

4. *Hope*

One of the most difficult aspects of grief is when hope dies. It may be hope for physical healing, but it also may be hope for healing of relationships or the hope of hearing a parent say they are proud of you or that they love you. As shaky as hope in this world's relationships is, we can have a grounded hope in the Living Hope.[79]

> *Psalm 16:8-9 I have set the LORD always before me: because he is at my right hand, I shall not be moved. Therefore my heart is g lad, and my glory rejoiceth: my flesh also shall rest in hope.*
>
> *Jeremiah 17:7-8 Blessed is the man that trusteth in the LORD, and whose hope the LORD is. For he shall be as a tree planted by the waters, and that spreadeth out her roots by the river, and shall not see when heat cometh, but her leaf shall be green; and shall not be careful in the year of drought, neither shall cease from yielding fruit.*

---

79   1 Peter 1:3-5 Blessed be the God and Father of our Lord Jesus Christ, which according to his abundant mercy hath begotten us again unto a lively hope by the resurrection of Jesus Christ from the dead, To an inheritance incorruptible, and undefiled, and that fadeth not away, reserved in heaven for you, Who are kept by the power of God through faith unto salvation ready to be revealed in the last time.

1 Peter 3:15 But sanctify the Lord God in your hearts: and be ready always to give an answer to every man that asketh you a reason of the hope that is in you with meekness and fear:

5. Minister

Each of us who have received comfort from the Father in any way have been given the ministry of comfort to others. When we begin to step outside of our own problems and minister to others we begin to fulfill our calling.

2 Corinthians 1:3-4 Blessed be God, even the Father of our Lord Jesus Christ, the Father of mercies, and the God of all comfort; Who comforteth us in all our tribulation, that we may be able to comfort them which are in any trouble, by the comfort wherewith we ourselves are comforted of God.

Galatians 6:1-2 Brethren, if a man be overtaken in a fault, ye which are spiritual, restore such an one in the spirit of meekness; considering thyself, lest thou also be tempted. Bear ye one another's burdens, and so fulfil the law of Christ.

6. Grow

Trials have a purpose and that is to grow us towards the Lord; to cause us to be more like Him. It would be sad if we were to endure a great trial and end on the other side the same as when we started.

Romans 8:28-29 And we know that all things work together for good to them that love God, to them who are the called according to his purpose. For whom he did foreknow, he also did predestinate to be conformed to the image of his Son, that he might be the firstborn among many brethren.

2 Corinthians 12:9-10 And he said unto me, My grace is sufficient for thee: for my strength is made perfect in weakness. Most gladly therefore will I rather glory in my infirmities, that the power of Christ may rest upon me. Therefore I take pleasure in infirmities, in reproaches, in necessities, in persecutions, in distresses for Christ's sake: for when I am weak, then am I strong.

7. Rest

God is our Rest. When life's difficulties beat us down we need to find a place of rest. God is that for His children.

Psalm 37:7 Rest in the LORD, and wait patiently for him: fret not thyself because of him who prospereth in his way, because of the man who bringeth wicked devices to pass.

Matthew 11:28 Come unto me, all ye that labour and are heavy laden, and I will give you rest.

Psalm 119:165 Great peace have they which love thy law: and nothing shall offend them.

Isaiah 26:3-4 Thou wilt keep him in perfect peace, whose mind is stayed on thee: because he trusteth in thee. Trust ye in the LORD for ever: for in the LORD JEHOVAH is everlasting strength:

There is nothing magical about the above steps, but God honors His people when they honor Him. Let us honor Him with our trust and our hope. Let us obey Him by passing along to others the many blessings He has bestowed upon us. When we do those things, we will find that our grief is lessened and our hope for tomorrow allows us to enter into His rest for today.

Plan of Salvation

For Those Who are not Saints

It is my hope that the previous chapters have provided comfort to God's children, both the ones who are facing their own death and those who have experienced the death of a loved one. However, none of what has been written prior to this offers any comfort to the person who does not know Jesus Christ as his personal Savior. One of the Scriptures used was *Psalm 116:15 "Precious in the sight of the Lord is the death of His saints."* The "saints" are the children of God who have accepted His work on the cross as payment for their sins.

Genesis, the first book of the Bible, records the story of Adam and Eve. God had created the heavens and the earth, separated darkness from light and created the animals, birds and fishes. He then created Adam in His own image out of the newly formed dust of the ground and breathed His life into Adam. God placed him in the Garden of Eden, telling Adam of the one tree in the entire garden that he could not eat of— the tree of the knowledge of good and evil. God also made woman, a help for Adam, and named her Eve.

Along with the instruction not to eat of the tree of knowledge of good and evil came a warning, 'in the day you eat of it' you *"will surely die."* (Genesis 2:17). Adam and Eve did eat of the fruit of the tree and were immediately aware of their sin. They sewed together leaves to cover their nakedness. Then they hid from God in shame. Part of the curse that came upon Adam and Eve and all of their descendants that day was physical death. Another part of the curse was that they were banished from the Garden of Eden. The intimate fellowship they had enjoyed with God ended. Romans 5:12 says *"Wherefore, as by one man sin entered into the world, and death by sin; and so death passed unto all men, for that all have sinned."* Our parents, Adam and Eve, passed the curse of sin down to every one of us.[80]

These two curses, physical death and separation from God, have followed mankind since that day in the Garden. However, God, in His infinite grace, made a way for the curse to turn to a blessing. *"For God so loved the world, that he gave his only begotten Son, that whosoever believeth in him should not perish, but have everlasting life." (John 3:16).*

There are a few simple steps to become a saint, a child of God. They are simple to follow but hard for the proud sinner to do.

First, recognize that you are a sinner.

> *For all have sinned, and come short of the glory of God. Romans 3:23*

God leaves no room for doubt. We ALL have sinned and we ALL fall short of the glory of God.

> *As it is written, "There is none righteous, no, not one." Romans 3:10*

Again it is plainly stated, none of us have a

---

80 Except for Jesus who was born of a virgin and had no earthly father.

righteousness of our own to commend us to God – not Billy Graham, not Mother Theresa, not you, not me.

Realize that there is a penalty for sin.

> For the wages of sin is death Romans 6:23a

Just as death followed Adam and Eve's sin so it follows ours. And just as part of the curse for Adam and Eve was separation from God, so it is for you and me as well.

Believe that God provided a payment of the penalty for your sin.

> But God commendeth his love toward us, in that, while we were yet sinners, Christ died for us. Romans 5:8

> But the gift of God is eternal life, through Jesus Christ our Lord. Romans 6:23b

This is a gift from God. It is not something we earn by our good works outweighing our sins.

> For by grace are ye saved, through faith; and not that of yourselves: it is the gift of God: not of works, lest any man should boast. Ephesians 2:8-9

Understand that we have to accept the gift.

It is not automatically given because we are good enough, nor does God force us to take the gift. We must accept it, asking Him to forgive us for our sins.

> For whosoever shall call upon the name of the Lord shall be saved. Romans 10:13

> That if thou shalt confess with thy mouth the Lord Jesus, and shalt believe in thine heart that God hath raised him from the dead, thou shalt

be saved. For with the heart man believeth unto righteousness; and with the mouth confession is made unto salvation. Romans 10:9-10

God says that if we honestly follow the steps above that He will save us and we will be one of His saints.

It is not a church, it is not a denomination, nor is it being raised in a good family that saves us.

Therefore being justified by faith, we have peace with God through our Lord Jesus Christ: By whom also we have access by faith into this grace wherein we stand, and rejoice in hope of the glory of God. Romans 5:1-2

He says once we are one of His saints there is no fear of condemnation.

There is therefore now no condemnation to them which are in Christ Jesus, who walk not after the flesh, but after the Spirit. Romans 8:1

He says that there is nothing that can separate His saints from Himself.

For I am persuaded, that neither death, nor life, nor angels, nor principalities, nor powers, nor things present, nor things to come, nor height, nor depth, nor any other creature, shall be able to separate us from the love of God, which is in Christ Jesus our Lord. Romans 8:38-39

Did you notice that there is <u>nothing</u> that can separate us from Him? The very first thing mentioned that cannot separate us from God is death! If we are one of His saints, our death will be precious in His sight. He will come to walk through the valley of the shadow of death with us—just as He did for both Moses and Stephen.

Heaven -Or- Hell

There are many who believe that all will go to heaven. We have been told that hell is a teaching left over from the old days. Many are too 'enlightened' now to believe what the Bible clearly teaches. They believe that God could not be a loving God and send anyone to hell.

The book of Revelation says that nothing will enter the new heaven that will defile it. This includes sinners who are not made clean by the work of Jesus Christ on Calvary. Only the ones whose names are written in the Lamb's book of Life will enter this land. *"And there shall in no wise enter into it any thing that defileth, neither whatsoever worketh abomination, or maketh a lie: but they which are written in the Lamb's book of life." Revelation 21:27.*

Some believe in hell, but believe it is reserved for people who did not do enough good works. It is common for people to say "I am sure that my good works will outweigh my bad works." God sent His Son to live on this earth as a pattern for our life. Jesus was crucified on a cross to die for our sins. God requires payment for sin, and only the perfect Son of God could make that payment. There are only two options left for us: accept Christ or reject Him.

In the book of Genesis, God says that Adam's and Eve's sin brought upon them, and then unto us, the curse of death. We have been living under this curse since that time. Unfortunately, some choose to live throughout eternity under that curse. For those who reject the work of Christ on the cross, the book of Revelation describes their judgment *"And I saw a great white throne, and him that sat on it, from whose face the earth and the heaven fled away; and there was found no place for them. And I saw the dead, small and great, stand before God; and the books were opened: and another book was opened, which is the book of life: and the dead were judged out of those things which were written in the books, according to their works. And the sea gave up the dead which were in it; and death and hell delivered up the dead which were in them: and they were judged every man according to their works. And death and hell were cast into the lake of fire. This is the second death. And whosoever was not found written in the book of life was cast into the lake of fire." Revelation 20:11-15.* Only the names of the saints are written in the Book of Life.

God will someday wipe away all tears and abolish death for His saints, *"And I heard a great voice out of heaven saying, Behold, the tabernacle of God is with men, and he will dwell with them, and they shall be his people, and God himself shall be with them, and be their God. And God shall wipe away all tears from their eyes; and there shall be no more death, neither sorrow, nor crying, neither shall there be any more pain: for the former things are passed away. And he that sat upon the throne said, Behold, I make all things new. And he said unto me, Write: for these words are true and faithful." Revelation 21:3-5.*

Revelation 22:3 says there will *"be no more curse."* The curse that came upon man in the book of Genesis will be done away with. The curse of death will be done away with. The curse of separation from God will be erased as the saints spend all of eternity with Him.

God will make all things new. He will abolish death, sorrow, crying and pain. The beautiful Garden of Eden, inhabited by the very presence of God, was a foreshadow of what was to come. But heaven is reserved only for the saints of God.

When we get to this point in the Biblical record there are no more chances to accept Christ's work, there is no more time to confess your need of a Savior, there is no more time to choose heaven over hell. *"He that is unjust, let him be unjust still: and he which is filthy, let him be filthy still: and he that is righteous, let him be righteous still: and he that is holy, let him be holy still"* Revelation 22:11. The unsaved will be unsaved forever and the saints will be saints forever.

It is up to you to decide whether to choose heaven with God or hell with the Devil and his demons. I hope and pray that you choose Jesus Christ. You can choose Him right now, before it is too late.

The next step is to find a good church where you can grow in your faith. This is something that you need to pray about, seeking the Lord's wisdom in helping you make that important decision.

Salvation

If you would like to accept Jesus Christ as your personal Saviour so you can be sure that you will go to heaven when you die, you can pray the following prayer.

> *God, I know that I am a sinner based on your word that I have just read. God, I understand that you sent your only Son Jesus Christ to die upon that cross and shed His blood for my sins. I am sorry for my sins and with my whole heart I accept Jesus Christ as my Saviour. I believe that He died, rose from the grave and is alive today. I desire for you to take over my life and I will serve you forever. Thank you Jesus for saving me.*

Signed: _____

It is not the prayer that saves you; it is the work of Jesus Christ on the cross of Calvary that pays the entire penalty for your sin.

If you pray this prayer, please contact me and share the good news. We will rejoice together. Karl Crawford: karl@pinetreeministries.org

Or you may use the address in the front of this book to send me a letter of what Jesus has done in your heart.

Made in the USA
Columbia, SC
23 February 2020